MW01046813

Single-Wing Football
with an
End Over

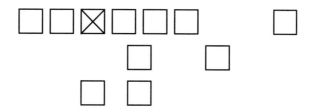

Bobby Anderson

Copyright © 2010 by Bobby Anderson

Single-Wing Football with an End Over
by Bobby Anderson

Printed in the United States of America

ISBN 9781609575939

All rights reserved solely by the author. The author guarantees all contents are original and do not infringe upon the legal rights of any other person or work. No part of this book may be reproduced in any form without the permission of the author. The views expressed in this book are not necessarily those of the publisher.

Unless otherwise indicated, Bible quotations are taken from the New King James Version. Copyright © 1982 by Thomas Nelson, Inc. Used by permission. All rights reserved.

www.xulonpress.com

Dedication

This book is dedicated to all those young men who were willing to come to two-a-day practice every August—to work hard, to have a dream, to become a team, to want to win, and to go through a rigid off-season program and pay that price that we always talk about. This book is dedicated to you, because without you there would be no book, and there would be no me.

Acknowledgements

Special gratitude goes to:

- Eddie Joseph—Executive Director THSCA and

- Mel Maxfield—Amarillo High School.

Special thanks go to:

- Joe Bob Tyler from Wichita Falls High School who probably taught me more about the single wing than anyone I have known;

- The University of Tennessee coaches Bowden Wyatt and Shirley Majors, a great high school coach in Huntland, Tennessee who later coached the University of the South;

- Tommy Prothro (Oregon State University; U.C.L.A) and Clay Stapleton (Iowa State University) who were great single-wing college coaches who learned under Henry (Red) Sanders of U.C.L.A.;

- Keith Piper from Dennison University in Ohio;

- Ed Racely, who gave me more material and encouraged me and helped me as a young coach more than almost anyone; and

- a very special thanks to Janet Stutts, one of my teaching comrades, who, out of the goodness of her heart wanted to type this manuscript for me and help me. I honestly do not believe she will ever know how much I appreciate it. Thank you, Janet.

Table of Contents

Forward xiii

A Player's Viewpoint xv

Chapter 1   Introduction: What This Manual Teaches 17

Chapter 2   Offensive Philosophy 22

Chapter 3   Why the Single Wing? Big Advantages! 28

     •   Offensive Philosophy 33

     •   Advantages of the Single Wing, Summarized 35

Chapter 4   How We Teach Our Single Wing 36

     •   Alignment 36

     •   Numbering System 37

     •   Formations—Right and Left 37

     •   Numbering 37

     •   Huddle 40

     •   Snap Count 42

Chapter 5   Line Play in the Single Wing Offense..................................43
- Personnel 43
- Center 43
- Guards 43
- Tackles 44
- Tight End 45
- Pre-Set 45
- Stances 45
- Drive Block 46
- Cut-off Block 47
- Drive-Turn Block 47
- Pulling 49

Chapter 6   Backfield Play in the Single-Wing Offense 53
- Personnel: Summary 53
- Personnel: Alignment 55
- Tailback 56
- Fullback 57
- Blocking Back 57
- Wingback 58
- Overview of Series 59

Chapter 7   Teen Series: Tailback Series to the Strong Side....................60
- Sweep 62
- 16 63
- Blast..64

- 15 Reverse 65

Chapter 8   Forty Series: Tailback Series and Quick Side 66
- 40 Trap 68
- 45 69
- Flicker Play 70

Chapter 9   Thirty Series: Fullback Quick Series 71
- Dive 74
- Wedge 75
- 37 Power 76

Chapter 10   Ninety Series: Fullback Spinner Series—the Best in All Football! 77
- Teaching the Fullback to Spin 79
- 96 85
- 94 86
- 90 Trap 87
- 95 Reverse 88
- 97 Reverse 89

Chapter 11   Pass Offense 90
- Pass Offense 90
- Split End/Split Receiver 91
- 18-Pass Routes 92
- 98 Pass 93
- Play Passes 93

•   Causes of Interceptions 95

Chapter 12   Variations and Special Plays 100

Chapter 13   Practice/Work-Out Schedule..103

Chapter 14   Strategy/Philosophy 104

Appendix A   Legend...107

Appendix B   Author's Biography 109

Forward

*T*his is the A-to-Z story of single-wing football as told by Bobby Anderson!

Inside this book is the complete story of the offense called the "single wing." It describes how it was and is played, told by a super successful Texas high school football coach. For twenty of his forty-three years he used this offense and is one of the very few coaches who still uses it. Step-by-step he gives you his own tips and pointers covering every phase of the single-wing offense.

In making this contribution to the great game of football, Coach Anderson hopes that everyone who reads this book will find something that proves to be of value.

There are very few football teams in high school or college who still use this offense; however, some of the very successful teams do run it. The author has tried to bring, bind, and blend together the facts, fundamentals, and philosophy of the single-wing offense.

For those who know and love football, it is a great read!

—Eddie Joseph, Executive President of the Texas High School
Coaches Association (THSCA) for many years
and a very good friend

As a reader and football coach, you are in for a treat! In this detailed book Coach Bobby Anderson will show his philosophy, concepts, and methods on coaching the single-wing offense. Coach Anderson's in-depth knowledge of the game and this offense will enhance your knowledge and understanding.

I have had the privilege of knowing Coach Anderson since the summer of 1991. What started out as a professional relationship quickly evolved into a life-long friendship. Bobby has had a major impact on my career. I have witnessed first-hand how to coach young men in the greatest game ever and how to help football players be all they can be—and a little more. Coach Anderson's trademark was rebuilding football programs, and he was certainly one of the best in the business in doing so. I encourage you to take advantage of the opportunity to learn from one of the best!

—Mel Maxfield, head football coach of Amarillo High School,

Amarillo, Texas, whom I had the good fortune to work for

and a very good friend

A Player's Viewpoint

*I*f I look back on my fifty-seven years on this earth, Coach Bobby Anderson would certainly be one of the top ten influential people in it. The same is no doubt true for hundreds and hundreds of other men, young and old, scattered across the state of Texas. These former high school football players had the unique honor to play under Coach Anderson for over forty years as his signature single-wing offense befuddled defenses far and wide.

With the hectic pace of modern life, we all too often fail to appreciate when our lives have truly been touched by something special. For many of us throughout Texas, that something special was Coach Anderson and all that he taught us—dedication, drive, perseverance, devotion to purpose, teamwork, and commitment. Hundreds of former high school football players had the unique honor to play under Coach Anderson for over forty years as his signature single-wing offense befuddled defenses far and wide.

For those of us in McGregor, Texas—just west of Waco—something very rare happened in 1968 and 1969. For you see, in 1967 the McGregor Bulldogs went 0 and 10 and barely scored any points. We were beyond down and out. And then Coach Anderson and two baby-faced young assistants, Gary Callaway and Bill Johnson, came to town and told us we were going to win district. We thought they were nuts! But they proceeded to teach us how not just to play, but also to truly play as a team. And in 1968 and 1969 those same McGregor Bulldogs won back-to-back district titles—defeating a previously undefeated Teague High School team my senior year in our last regular-season game in 1969.

As I write this, the City of McGregor is preparing to celebrate 100 years of Bulldog High School football. How appropriate then that Coach Anderson has written this book (as he approaches his 80th birthday) as his fine work united a small town with a sense of pride that is still very evident today. His former players include not only numerous valedictorians, but many high school coaches, teachers, doctors, lawyers, and business executives, from Odessa to Houston and beyond. He taught us well. So I recommend this book to all who wish to learn from him and to share in something special. And who knows, if you ever attend a McGregor High School football game on a cold and clear November night, in the stands you might just bump into one of the best there ever was—Coach Bobby Anderson. Tell him hello for me and for all the rest of the guys, and remind him that it was truly special.

—William Wade, attorney-at-law who played center for Coach Anderson
and was valedictorian of McGregor High School in 1969-70

Chapter 1

Introduction: What This Manual Teaches

In a nutshell, this manual is about the single-wing offense *with an end over*. The end-over look is used to aid the passing game while keeping the power running attack. This alignment makes the defense decide if we are balanced or unbalanced. If the defense over shifts, the quick-side corner is easy to attack. If the defense does not over shift, they are outmanned on the strong side.

Called today by names like the wild cat, the single wing by any other name smells as sweet. Football goes in cycles. Formations have gone from the split T to the wing T to the I formation to the wishbone to the split-back veer, to the spread, and then have mingled back and forth. Interest today in the pure single wing is spreading like fire. Simply put, our single wing *with an end over* leads to winning football games!

In the last several years, people have come up to me from time to time and told me, "You need to write a book on the offense you're running, because I think people would be interested in seeing what it is." When they said that, I thought about it and thought, "I don't know why, because the single wing is not a big offense that's in vogue today; it's not popular. I don't know why they'd want to see a book on it, and I'm not sure if I can do that or not." But as the time went by I would get questions again and again, "Are you ever gonna write a book on this?" So I did a little research.

I have been in the coaching profession a long time and have seen many, many, many good books about football—defense, the kicking game, the passing game, the running game, and all kinds of formations. I want to make one thing really clear about what this book will tell or what it will show. All my lifetime in the game of football as a coach or as a player, I never had one inno-vative idea. I do not say that to sound like I am trying to be humble or trying to just let it pass by. I do not have that kind of mind. I cannot imagine new formations, new offenses, or new plays. I have drawn those up and done that, but that is just not my way. I began to realize as I started to do this book that people are going to ask me many, many times, and I have been asked so many times, "Why do you run the single wing?" "Why the single wing?" "Where did you get that?" And so forth. This book is the answer.

I got it years ago. When I was playing, we played one or two good single-wing teams that just beat the daylights out of us, and we thought we had a good team. I want this book to simply tell what our single wing is about, because I discovered that in all the years with all the good books I've read (and there have been some great ones on football, including some great single-wing books), I have never seen one on the balanced line with an end over. I have never seen a book on it.

Many colleges ran the balanced line single wing and sent me their play books and films. The University of Tennessee Coach Bowden Wyatt did that. So did Coach Tommy Prothro with Oregon State University, Bill Barnes at UCLA, Clay Stapleton at Iowa State, and even some of the coaches at smaller colleges like Keith Piper at Dennison University, Shirley Majors at Huntland High School in Tennessee and the University of the South. They all had great single-wing offenses, but nobody wrote a book on it. And I started thinking about that. We added one thing on our single wing in the latter years that we did not run early and that was the end-over formation. By taking our left end and putting him as a split end on the right side, then switching the tight end to the left side, we had a really balanced-line strong side plus a good passing game. That is what we really thought helped us in the single wing—the end over.

When I said that I had never had an innovative idea, that is the absolute truth. I could take what I saw someone else do and do it…and try to do it as well as they did. There are a lot of good offenses. In my career I ran the wing T and the single wing. Our blocking stayed much the same.

But I always came back to the single wing. That was the thing that I seemed to enjoy most, and we had success with it.

Formations, everyone knows, do not win football games. Formations will allow you to use your players to their abilities sometimes more than others. But as a very young coach I was told something very important by a man whom I considered as good a football coach as ever lived—Coach Gordon Wood from Brownwood, Texas. In his many years of coaching he won eight state championships, if you can imagine that! Two were in Stamford, Texas and six in Brownwood. I heard Coach Wood lecture in clinic one time, and he said, "If I were giving any advice to a young coach, it would be, 'Stay out of the middle of the stream.'" What he meant was that if everybody you play runs the same thing you're running, or you run what everybody else you're gonna play against runs, familiarity is very easy to come about. He said, "You need something that's different."

I talked to him a lot of times through the years. He said, "You've got something different." And we did, because people just don't run the single wing any more. Right now the big rage in college and high school football is the spread. Probably every defensive coordinator in college or high school has spent the summer, all spring, days and nights, and other times, looking at a new way to defend the spread—something different that our defense can throw at them that they're not used to seeing. I doubt seriously if there's one defensive coordinator or head coach in America that's spent all this time trying to figure out a way, asking "Now how do we defend that single wing that we play only one time a year?"

That "stay out of the middle of the stream" really hit me. Coach Wood also said in that lecture that one of his friends told him in the off-season, "I'm changing to the I formation next year," which was a very good formation. Coach Wood said, "Why?" "Because all the teams in the bowl games ran the I." Coach Wood said, "All the teams that *lost* in the bowl games ran the I also!"

It's not *what* you run. It's *how* you run it. Get something that's sound and something you do. The spread is a great offense. I've played against it the last five years. And defensive people do different things against the spread. I've seen people that rush three people and drop eight off in the secondary. We're getting down to defense, but I'm trying to tie all this together to show you what our book will explain. We're going to show you in our book with our single-wing attack how we attack each defense. We *don't have blocking rules*. Everyone has blocking rules, and they all work. Every one of those blocking rules says, "Do this or this *unless* they do that," and everybody we play seems to run the "unless" on defense. We have a way that we block the odd defense. We have a way that we block the even. Simple.

One of the main reasons we run the single wing is that we felt like it gave us a little bit of an advantage to be different. When you got ready to play us, you couldn't just go out there and say, "Okay, they run this and this, and we'll get in our regular defense and slant or stunt or do what have you...." It's not that simple. In all my years of coaching, I noticed that when I first moved into a school, almost everybody we played looked at each other and said, "They can't run that stuff on us. They just can't run that on us."

Of course after we *did* run it on them, and if we won and had a good year (we had that a lot of times), the next year, those coaches went out and looked for every old single-wing coach they could find that was still alive and asked him, "How would you defend the single wing?"

The second year we played in that conference we saw every kind of crazy defense. There's nothing you could put there today that I have not seen. In every kind of defense that you could see, some of the things did work. But most of the time, you cannot put in a defense in just three days.

Normally, by the third year, they went back to their regular defense and adjusted it, which is, I think, as good as any. People have asked me, "How would you defend your single wing?" I've always said, "I don't know." And I don't! I've only played against one single-wing team, and they were an unbalanced line. So I'm not sure how. One thing that bothers us, more than anything, is not where your people line up. But we're interested in two things: Do you have a nose guard? Or do you slide over with us and cover our end-over side like we're unbalanced? But we'll get into that in a later chapter.

This book, I hope, will completely show you our formation, our numbering system, and the four different series that we run (Teen, Forty, Thirty, and Ninety). Our numbering system is not the best in the world, but for us it is good, and we know it. We do flip flop our formations right and left.

The single wing gives us another thing. Our single wing is good on our own one-yard line, or even on their one-yard line. We don't need to change formations. And our single wing is the very same on their one-yard line, ninety-nine yards down the field. We don't have to have a goal-line formation. We can run everything from that one formation we are in. We are in a goal-line offense all over the field. But we can also throw the ball from that same offensive anywhere on the field. And we have a power running game and great misdirection counter plays all from *one* formation.

I hope this book will show you that the single wing can be good at any level. I have seen it work well in high school. I have seen it work well in colleges. And I have seen it work on middle-school level well too. The biggest thing that is probably a problem for coaches today is that the blocking system they use in the spread is not what we run; it is not what the single wing is. We still have that power blocking, the double-team blocks, the traps, and the pulling-people-through-the-hole strategy. This is part of our offense, which I think really makes the offense what it is.

Chapter 2

Offensive Philosophy and Strategy
of a Winning Offence

We want to run a few things and run them almost perfectly. The other end of that spectrum is a group of coaches that love to run many formations, many plays, have many ideas, and give you something different to look at each week. But the thing I want to talk about here more than anything is that I am not trying to sell you anything. I simply made the decision to write this book, and if you get one or two things out of it that will help you in some way, it will have been worthwhile. I mainly want to express to you my feelings and my experience with the single-wing offense and the philosophy that we followed—the way we think one should play the game—so you will have a better chance to win.

In the forty some-odd years that I have been involved with football coaching, I have seen six major styles of offense come and go. Coaches are the biggest copycats in the world. We are all looking for something different, and we are all watching the people who win, seeing what they run, and wanting to run it like them. When I first started coaching, everyone was running the Split-T formation that The University of Oklahoma and Bud Wilkerson had such great success with. And that is what we ran.

The University of Iowa put in what they call the Delaware Wing-T formation. They got it from Dave Nelson and the University of Delaware. They wrote a book about it—an excellent coaching book. Iowa won the Rose Bowl with the wing T, and everybody in the country was trying to hurry and find out what the wing T was. That was the next system I saw come along—first the straight T, then the wing T.

The next offense that exploded in the nation was the I formation. John McKay at Southern Cal and Woody Hayes at Ohio State and the University of Michigan put it in. The I formation was the rage. Everybody changed to the I. The split T, the wing T and the I formation were the three major offenses I saw early in my coaching years. There were little wrinkles you could run off of all of them. You could run different kinds of wing T's. You could run the way Iowa or Delaware ran it, or you could run what they called the "Flip-Flop Wing T" where the strong side and the quick side switched places, depending on the formation you were in—right or left. The University of Texas won a national championship with that.

Things stayed the same for a while with the I formation and the wing T with a few people still running the straight T (the split T). Then along came the wishbone formation. I remember going to watch three outstanding high school teams in the state of Texas—Houston Stratford, Lewisville, and Southlake Carroll—all football powerhouses, all winning state championships running the wishbone. They ran it so well, when leaving the stadium after watching one of those teams play, I would wonder, "Why isn't everybody doing that?!" And they dominated for a good while.

Then Bill Yoeman at the University of Houston came in with the split-back veer offense and it was unbelievable. Everybody went to the veer. So with the split T, the wing T, the I formation, and the veer, people went back and forth between these offenses. Then the spread formation came and just exploded on the football world. Everybody was then going to the spread formation.

Those are offenses I saw over that forty some-odd year period. And every one of them was a great offense. That old cliché that "offense wins games, defense wins championships" is very true. But something else is very important—the kicking game. Your kickoff, your kickoff return, your punting game, your punt return, your extra point field goal—all of that is an important part of winning.

Now to get to our basic philosophy One of the first things I learned about offense as a player and a coach was a strategy of ball control, field position, working the clock, and keeping the other team's best passer, best runner, and best receiver standing on the sideline drinking Gatorade. Because if we have the ball and they do not have it, they cannot get on the field to play very much. That was very important to all of us—field position and clock management and keeping the football. We love to make those *long*, sustained drives. I have reel after reel and can after can of films, and now DVD's, that show us making seventy-five or eighty-yard drives and taking anywhere from seven to nine minutes in a quarter to do it. We just dominated with ball control.

When you talk about ball control, people say, "That's boring football. I like to see the passing game." I know this, you *have* to throw the football to win. Many people did not think the wishbone threw the football. And some did not. But I assure you that The University of Alabama with Coach Bryant threw it and ran it well. The high school teams I saw could do it too. People who say ball control is boring want to throw every down and have a touchdown pass or a lateral off the ball. Some people do this and have success with it. But our system is to control the ball, run the football, and throw the football when we *want* to and not when we *have* to. But we want to be able to make those long drives. To me, when I look at the scoreboard at the end of the game, and we have more points than they do…that's *not* boring! It's just my personality in my offense. I don't want to play in a game where we win sixty-two to fifty-four. And we have had that in Texas. To me that is like watching a ping-pong match. In football, defense is important. If you are going to control the ball, you have to have an attacking defense that can take the ball away and get it back. Football should not be a scoring contest when you do not even work on defense—they score, you try to score, they score, and the one who scores last is going to win the game.

The spread has been tremendously successful. I know a coach who changed to the I formation, because all the bowl teams that won ran the I. His friend told him that all the bowl teams that *lost* ran the I too! The spread is that way. Those spread teams that score lots of points and get lots of points scored against them do not always win. I am not here to knock anybody's offense. That is not my purpose. Whatever you have for an offense, you like and believe in, so do not change anything. Do not jump around. Get something you believe in and run it well.

That is basically our strategy and philosophy. We will be able to throw the football. We have lots of long runs. But I like to take it and just keep the football and let the clock run. That panics a lot of people on the other side, because they say they are not getting the ball very much. To me, that is an important part of football.

Football games are determined many, many times not by what you do but by the *mistakes* the other team makes or the mistakes that you sometimes make. Mistakes can determine games. There is not an offense in football that is not going to make mistakes. I was told when I first went to the single wing that we had better have a good center or two. We always had two every year. In those twenty years we ran the single wing, we never lost a game because of a bad snap. That snap did not cost us a football game. We lost games with other things. We lost games because we did not play defense well enough, someone got a penalty on a crucial play, or something like that. But I think you should get an offensive philosophy you believe in and not change it. Stay with what you do. That is what we did. In the thirty-three years I was a head coach, I ran the single wing twenty years. I look back now and wish I had run it for all the rest of them! But every time we thought we would not have the personnel for something, we would switch.

I am probably not very bright, the way I let my coaching career go, because I took the jobs that no one else or very few people wanted. I took the *down* jobs. The people who were down and getting beaten over and over wanted somebody to come in and put a program in. That is the thing I enjoyed doing. In those twenty years, that is what I did with the single wing. During the other years I coached we ran a wing T, and our blocking stayed much the same as the single wing, but it was just not the same.

I have read countless philosophies, and they sound just as good as or better than ours. But this one was the one I thought I could make work. This one was the one that proved it did. This helped us take programs that were down and put them in a place where they either won or tied their football district and got in the playoffs. Out of twenty years, we did that sixteen times. That was in the day when only one team went to the playoffs instead of three or four like we do now. If it had been two teams back then, we would have gone to the playoffs eighteen times out of those twenty years. It worked well for us.

Offensive Football

Outside Plays

Sweep (TB)

Flicker (WB)

37 (FB)

Misdirection Plays

15R (WB)

95R (WB)

97R (WB)

Trap Plays

40 Trap (TB)

90 Trap (FB)

Special Plays

Jump Pass

97 Reverse Pass

BB Down the Middle

Screen Pass

TE Special

Curl & Pitch

Passes

18 Passes

98 Passes

Power Plays

Dive (FB)

Wedge (BB)

Blast (TB)

Off-Tackle Plays

16 (TB)

96 (TB)

94 (FB)

45 (TB)

Chapter 3

Why the Single Wing?

I have probably been asked this question hundreds of times. And many times it is asked in the connotation that there is something wrong with it. People ask, "Why in the world are you doing that?" Other times they ask, "Where did you get that?" And other times, again, it is asked by people who have already made their mind up with, "I don't like that single wing, and I don't know why in the world you run it."

Almost every coach can give you the reasons he runs his offense. I have heard coaches say we run a formation that fits our personnel. I heard a great coach say one time, "If you do that, it means you have no continuity at all. You're changing the formation in your offense every year to fit your personnel." I was advised years ago, and thank Goodness someone told me this, to find a formation that will fit *any* personnel. You know the kind of person you have to have playing each position. And he just gets to be the best he can be on that position. Then you have a constant stream of seventh graders who learn that, then play in eighth grade and learn more, then go into the ninth grade and into the tenth and on up learning even more.

The single wing is not that hard to *teach*. It *is* hard to *defend*. Unless your personnel is just totally way above ours, it does not make any difference what the formation is, you are going be able to defend most anything you see.

In another part of our book I have ten advantages of the single wing. But here, I would like to tell you that coaches are the most fashion-conscious group of people I have ever known. Oh, I know women are conscious about fashion. But coaches! We are all the same; we are copycats. Someone comes along and does something different and has great success. Everybody wants to know, "What was that?" and "How'd they do it?" Then they jump on the bandwagon.

When I was a player in college, you ran two things. We ran Bud Wilkinson's split-T offense like Oklahoma. Well, we didn't run it like Oklahoma, but we *tried* to. Or we ran Bobby Dodd's Georgia Tech belly series. If you weren't running those two things, you were outdated and just not with it. Every coach we played against ran that, and of course we ran it in college. When I got out of college in my first job as an assistant coach, I knew the split T, and I knew the option plays. (I was an option quarterback.) I knew the belly series, so they hired me to coach the backs, and we'd run that. When I took my first head-coaching job, I put the same thing in, and we won our first game. In our second game, we won it. But in the third game, our quarterback, who also played safety on defense (because we were a small school), intercepted a pass, returned it about thirty-five to forty yards down to about the other team's twenty-yard line, and they tackled him. He didn't get up. When I got out there, we called for a doctor. He had broken his collarbone. Of course they had to take him to the hospital.

Being a first-year coach and thinking I was organized, I now had no idea what to do. I remember I had taught a young sophomore to take the snap from center and run the hand-off play to either side, so he could go in and rest our good quarterback when and if we got way ahead. So now I put this young man in to replace our injured quarterback, and that's what we ran. At the halftime we tried to teach him a couple of other things. We ended up getting beaten—six to nothing. We just couldn't move the ball at all. And all along I had thought about the single wing. So I decided we would put it in the very next week. We put in six plays with the single wing. We worked on our center and kept him after practice for extra work on his snap. We had a good football team. We had some good athletes. And we won the next twenty football games in a row! In two years, we were twenty-three and one. I thought I had found the magic formula!

However, the only thing I knew about the single wing was the kind of single wing that I had seen Tennessee run—the draw series. They call it the ride series today. That was our beginning; that is what put us in the single wing. I know we would not have won it had we put in the young man we tried to play as quarterback. He ended up being a great, little wingback and blocking back. That is how we got into the single wing.

Then I changed schools and moved to a larger school. The next three years we won with it again—three good winning seasons. By that time I had begun to pick up other ideas, and I had begun to call coaches, and I had begun to write coaches. The Wichita Falls coach at that time, a gentleman named Joe Golding, gave me some information I needed. One of his assistants, Joe Bob Tyler, helped me a whole lot. I learned about the fullback-spinner series (Ninety Series). And that became our *number-one* series that we still run. I can confidently say now that without the Ninety Series, I would not run the single wing, period.

That is the way we got into the single wing; we were forced into it by an injury. We ran it twenty-two years! Every now and then we would look and say, "Well we do not have this or that certain position." So we would run a strong-set wing T. Gordon Wood and his coaches at Brownwood High School called their wing T nothing but a single wing with a quarterback under the center. I thought it was a whole lot more than that, because I saw them play. We would run that wing T some, and then I would always come back and run the single wing.

Let me tell you why I think the single wing is an advantage. If you are running the balanced-line single wing (or the unbalanced), and you're the only team in your district that runs it, and there's nobody on your schedule that runs it, and you can't even find anybody within *a hundred miles* that runs it, you *are* going to give the people you play against a big problem. They're going to have to get ready for you in three days and get their defense going and that's hard to do in three days. You cannot make our single wing in practice look like it looks on game night. You can put in an assistant coach to run the spinner series, and you can do all that, and he may be good, but it's just not the same. You don't get the picture of the speed of it. And you don't get the picture of what it looks like when the thing really runs smoothly and has been practiced and practiced. We want it to look just like a machine when it does that, so it will give the other team a problem.

One of the disadvantages of running the single wing is that we know what they run on defense, and that's what we'll practice against. But most of them changed it on us during that week and came out with a brand-new defense, and we had to quickly make sideline adjustments. We got to the place where we could do just that, but that is one of the things that gives you a headache offensively.

Another advantage we think we have in the single wing is the fact that we can both run and throw the football from just *one* formation. A lot of people used to run the wing T and throw the ball well. They'd spread the weak side end and run it. Our end over has helped our running game to the strong side more than *anything*. We feel that in our formation we can run the ball with power, we can run it with deception, reverses, and spinner series, and we have the best running pass in football. The NFL teams and the college teams will pitch a ball back to a halfback or tailback, and he will throw a pass. When we throw the running pass, our passer is throwing the ball. We also can flood a zone better with ours. We have great passing attack away from the split end. And in a bootleg series, we throw off of our reverses; we have play passes from that. The single wing is a great formation from which to both run and throw the football.

There is one last thing I want to mention about our single wing formation. Almost everybody thinks their offense answers all their questions, or they would not be running it. Probably the biggest advantage the single wing has, and I think there are many of them, is that you do not have to have great big, strong players. We have a few. But a small lineman that can run and who is tough can play in the single wing. We'd rather have those than have those great big ones that can't move. Now if we can get a big one that can move, then we've really got what we need. But our linemen, every one of them, with one exception, have to learn to pull to the right or the left. So we have to have people that can move.

Another thing.... I know people who when you tell them you can play small linemen, they start thinking, "Well, you're not going to be able to block anybody on the goal line or in short-yardage situations." We're going to be able to block people in *every* situation we face, because we are going to teach the double-team block to *every* lineman that plays for us. They are going to perfect that, and you can move people, because two can block one. We also use pulling and trapping with our linemen, and we pull our linemen to go through the hole and block linebackers. And quicker people have to play those positions. When we show you how we set our offense up, we'll explain who has to be the largest and who can be the smallest, who has to pull this way, and who has to pull that way. Pulling linemen, double-team blocking, and people in front of the football are the real advantage of the running game in the single wing.

Let me close this chapter by saying that we believe very strongly in our offensive system. Like I said before, all coaches do. You have to do that if you are ever going to be successful. But we also are smart enough to know how true that the old cliché is—"Offense will win games; defense will win championships." To be a solid football team, you have to have an offense that can both run and throw the football. You have to have a defense that can stop the offensive on the other team. And you have to have a sound kicking game. We don't think we have the answer of how to do that. We think we have the answer for us, and we have the answer for our system and for our coaching staff for the things we want to teach each one of our teams.

Offensive Philosophy

1. Have a <u>system</u> you understand and believe in (i.e. single wing).

2. <u>Do not beat yourself</u>. This philosophy can be taught. Eliminate turnovers.

3. Have a play you can "hang your hat on." Ours is not one but two plays, the <u>Sweep</u> and the <u>Blast</u>. Execute these plays so well that the opponent has to spend extra time defending them. Do not be hard headed; they will not always be our best plays and will usually be better in the second half.

4. <u>Be able to throw the football</u>. When playing teams of equal talent or better, it can be the difference between winning and losing.

5. Be prepared. <u>Make sideline adjustments</u> during the game if the other team has changed their defense.

6. <u>Execution</u> is the key to successful offense. Simplify the offense as much as possible. Don't have so much offense that the players cannot execute.

7. Have a <u>pre-determined</u> play to open the game and always have a well-planned game plan. Know what plays you will call for all down and distance situations. Get the feel of the game. Never just grab bag. Adjust during the game.

8. <u>Never give up on your players</u>. Always stay positive with them.

9. Practice a <u>two-point play each week</u>. Sell the players that it might be the difference in the game!

10. Have a <u>trick play</u> each week. We might need it to get back into the game or change the momentum. It also puts some fun into the game for the players! ☺

Advantages of the Single Wing

1. The single wing can get more blockers in front of the ball carrier than any other formation.

2. Small linemen can be used because double-team blocking and pulling are the basis of this attack.

3. The split receiver gives the advantage of the shotgun.

4. The tailback can be a great runner and an average passer (or vice-versa).

5. Great misdirection is used in the single wing.

6. This offense is impossible to prepare for in three or four days. There is no way to show your team the true picture that they will see on game night.

7. The single wing is a great formation from which to throw the ball.

8. The Play Pass Series and Running Pass Series are the best from the single wing.

9. The Fullback Spinner Series is the *finest* series in all of football!

10. The end-over alignment forces the defense to make a decision: are we balanced or unbalanced?

Chapter 4

How We Teach the Single Wing

Alignment

The first decision we have to make is determining what positions certain personnel will play. The first time we meet to talk to them about it, we want everyone to be sure and know what position we are going to assign them to start with. We may move their position, but we are going to play them where we need them. We are going to start out and put them in the places where we think they can probably do the best job. This is the only way I know to do it—to show the numbering system.

Once we show them the positions, we show them the right formations. We will take a tight end and put him there, then take a quick-side guard, a center, a strong-side guard, an inside tackle, and an outside tackle, and we will show them their alignment on the line of scrimmage. We will also show our split receiver his alignment outside the outside tackle on the line, and we will show you where he lines up—anywhere from eight to ten yards wide.

A lot of people, I understand, let people try out for certain positions. We have never done that. We feel, as coaches, we can look at people and, through drills and practice, find out who could probably play certain positions. I have found that some of the coaches who let people try out say that when they got through, they did not have anything but quarterbacks and wide receivers! The game of football is made up of eleven different people. In every offence (and the single wing is particularly dependent on this) every position on that offense has certain skills and certain things that the players must do. You take the people who fit those skills and those things they must do, and you put them in that place. We may change after the first practice, we may change after five weeks, or we may change after the first fifteen minutes. But we are going to move people around until we feel like we have the eleven best people playing in the right positions to make our offense go.

Numbering System

After we teach the alignment like this, we teach the numbering system. We have even numbers on the strong side and odd numbers on the quick side. (We used to call that the weak side, but you do not call anybody playing on your football team weak!) On our quick side, our tight end is the five hole. Our quick-side guard is the three hole. Our center is the zero hole. Our strong-side guard is the two hole. The inside tackle is the four hole. And the outside tackle is the six hole. Outside the outside tackle is the eight hole. We have numbers two, four, six and eight on the strong side. We have zero, three, five, and seven on the quick side. Later we will explain about the people who will play these positions and the skills they need.

Formations—Right and Left

After we teach the linemen where to line up in the right formation, we take our backs and place them in the right formation. Our tailback, or our quarterback, as he is sometimes called, plays four yards straight behind the center. We will talk about stances later. Remember, we do not number backs in the single-wing offense. Our fullback (or running back, as he is sometimes called) lines up almost behind the quick-side guard and is probably about six inches, maybe a heel-toe relationship, in front of the tailback. They do line up even a lot of times, depending on what plays we are running. I used to think if we moved them six inches, the defense would know what we were doing. But I found out that it is not that way. It would be nice for the defense if it were, but it does not make any difference whether they are even or six inches apart. They can run all of our plays from either of those spots.

Our blocking back, who is for us the man who calls our snap count, lines up in the gap between the strong-side guard and the quick-side tackle. Our wingback lines up about two feet back from the outside tackle and two feet outside of him. That is our basic right formation single wing!

We only run two formations to start with, the right formation and the left formation. We have given you the right formation. You can see from the diagrams the numbers on the strong side and the numbers on the quick side. You see the spacing, about six inches between each lineman. And you know how deep the backs line up and what they do.

The classic single-wing line

Alignment, Numbering, Right and Left Formation

Right Formation

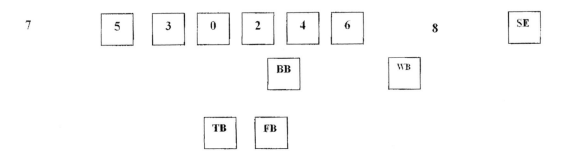

Left Formation 7

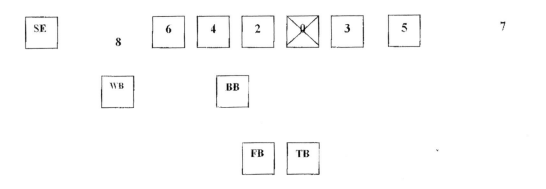

Line Splits

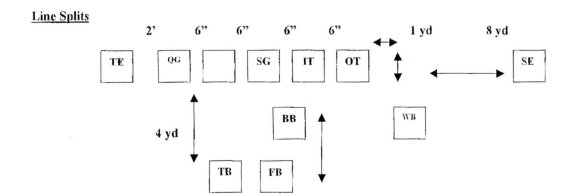

The Huddle

This is the simplest way I know how to huddle. We have a huddle that we can come straight out of and be lined up in a right formation. But since we also run a left formation, we have the same huddle and we can *serpentine* out of it. The diagram is a little confusing, but we can explain it in about thirty seconds on the field. If our play caller calls left formation, our outside tackle in the huddle knows immediately he is going to come and bend around to his left, and he is going to end up over on the opposite side of where he was a while ago. All the linemen follow him all the way around. So for a left formation, our tight end is now over here on the right side, our quick side guard is now over here on the right side, our center is still in the zero hole, our strong-side guard is in the two hole on this side now, our inside tackle is the four hole, and our outside tackle is the six hole. Outside of that wide is the eight hole. We have flipped the numbers, but we have also flipped the players with them, which means we can run twice as much offense, and players only have half the assignments to learn!

It sounds complicated and it does not look good drawn up. I have tried every way in the world to draw it up, but I can explain it to you by *serpentining*. Our outside tackle knows that if he hears "right formation," the whole team just comes straight up the line and lines up in right formation. If he hears "left formation," he knows he is going to serpentine out and end up on the quick side (left side), and we swap the holes. Our wingback will go behind the huddle to line up, and our split receiver will go behind the huddle if it is a left formation.

It sounds complicated. But once you have done it three or four times, it is not complicated. This is the simplest way I have found. It is a lot easier than crossing in the huddle and lining up different ways. It is for me.

Our huddle is hard to visualize on paper. But it is simple to us, because we have used it so long. We have an open huddle facing the defense. When we come out of left formation, we serpentine out with all the linemen, so we don't step on each other or run in front of each other. It is really simpler to teach than it looks.

Huddle

Right

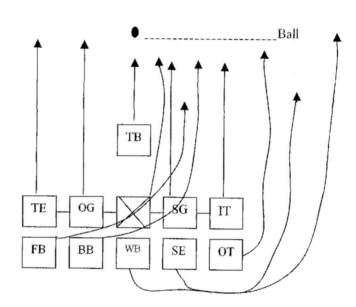

Left

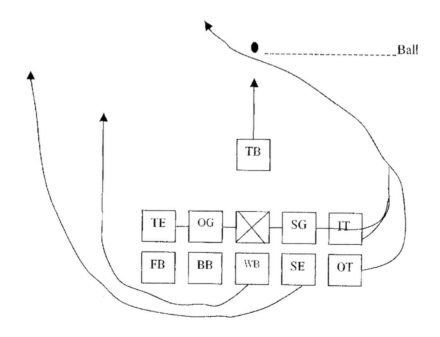

Snap Count

When we come to the line of scrimmage we all get down in what we call a pre-set stance. We are down with our elbows resting on our thighs with nice, balanced feet. Our quarterback will come up to the line of scrimmage and say, "Set." When he does, everyone puts his right hand down. I do not care if you are left handed, right handed, or both handed. We all put our right hands down. Our strong-side guard puts his right hand down six inches behind the football. The quick-side guard does the same. And the linemen put their hands down, lined even with the man inside them.

Once we come up to the line, we are in a pre-set stance. Our quarterback will say "Set," and all the backs except the quarterback and the fullback will put their hands on the ground right along with the linemen. The blocking back and the wingback have the same three-point stance that the linemen have. But when he says that, the quarterback and the fullback just open their hands up like they are ready to catch the snap.

The formations are diagrammed. Once you do it and see it a few times, it becomes a good habit.

Chapter 5

Line Play in the Single Wing Offense

Personnel: Front 7

Center (C)

- He must be smart and consistent. (During the 26 years we ran the single wing, eight of our centers were valedictorian or salutatorian of their class.)
- The number-one job of our center is to snap the ball perfectly every time.
- Size and speed are not a factor.
- Snapping the ball is a skill that *can be taught*.

Quick Guard (QG)

- He must be strong enough to gap block and drive turn with the center or the TE on 5-hole plays.
- He must be a good cutoff blocker.
- He must have speed to get in front of the sweep.
- He pulls and seals the 6-hole and blocks through the 4-hole.
- He is usually the smallest and quickest lineman.

Strong Guard (SG)

- Most of the time we pick our best lineman to play SG.
- Size and speed (quickness) are important.
- Our SG pulls to the strong side and the quick side.
- He must be a great drive blocker, cutoff blocker, and drive-turn blocker.
- He is a leader and *key* to the single wing.

Inside Tackle (IT)

- He is usually our biggest lineman.
- He needs to be a strong drive blocker.
- Speed is not a key factor.
- One of the real advantages of our single wing is having twin tackles playing side by side (inside and outside).
- Our inside tackle must be a great cutoff and drive-turn blocker.

Outside Tackle (OT)

- He is the *second* player picked for the front seven.
- He needs some size and speed—enough to pull and lead all 5-hole and 7-hole reverses (15R-95R-97R).
- He should be a good cutoff blocker and a good drive-turn blocker on the 4-hole and 6-hole (94-16-96).
- He is usually a good (versatile) athlete that plays other sports.

Split End (SE)

- He needs to be an athlete.
- He needs speed to go deep.

- He needs great hands (best receiver).

- He must develop the skill of running perfect pass routes.

- We usually play three or four split ends.

Tight End (TE)

- He is the *first* player picked for the front seven.

- He needs to have good hands.

- He is a good receiver.

- He must be a great cut-off and drive-turn blocker.

- Size is nice but not critical.

- He plays a big role in our passing game.

- He is a key blocker that makes our 5-hole and 7-hole plays work.

Guard, tackle, and tight end's three-point stance and pre-set stance

Guard and center lined up at center and lined up in three-point stance

Drive Block

The drive block is the first and most important thing we teach in our offense. We are a shoulder-blocking football team. We do not butt people in the face with our helmets. We do not push people with our hands. We are a *shoulder-blocking* football team.

All of our linemen are required to learn three blocks. The first one is the *drive block*. That is our shoulder block, where we block one on one—the man in front of us. We learn that block on stand-up dummies. We have a line painted on that dummy; you cannot raise your head above that line. We have to stay low. We try to teach everyone to drive block by himself the best he can. I have never had a football team—and I have had some good ones—where every lineman on it could not drive block anybody lined up in front of him. It did not make any difference who he was, *every* lineman could block anyone in front of him. That does not happen often! Even in the NFL, it does not happen.

Cut-Off Block

The next block we teach is the *cut-off block*. We are a shoulder-blocking football team, but this block is totally different. A lot of people criticize this block because they think you are going to hurt someone. We have used the cut-off block forty-five years running the single wing, and we have *never, ever* hurt anyone with it! Not one. It is *not* a crack-back block. It is not a block where you are trying to take his feet out from under him. You are trying to throw that block, shoot that inside arm outside of him, and get down and scramble block him. What you are trying to do on the cut-off block is to keep the man you are blocking from going out where the hole is. We teach this on a stand-up dummy as we do with the drive block.

Drive-Turn Block

The other block we teach is the *drive turn block,* which is the double team. That is the *foundation* of the single-wing offense—the double-team block. The drive block is the shoulder block. The cut-off block gets your head and shoulders past the guy down on all fours and scrambling to keep him from going where the ball is. But the last block is the backbone and every other kind of bone in the single wing, because it is the thing that makes it go.

We have small linemen play for us a lot of times who can run and who are tough as they can be. And they cannot block one-on-one for a full quarter or two quarters or three, and certainly not four, and block everybody perfectly. It is our firm belief that two people can block one. I do not care who the one is. Now when we say double-team block, that does not tell you a thing except two of us are going to block somebody. But *how* you block it is going to be the most important thing.

In teaching the drive-turn block let us start over on our quick side where the tight end is. He is the five hole. If we call a five-hole play, whether it is a 45, a 35, a 65, a 25, or a 16,400,085!, it is a five-hole play. The five hole is what we are blocking. When we hear that, our tight end knows immediately that he is going to drive turn block with our quick-side guard. Or if there is nobody down in front of our quick-side guard, then he knows the drive turn is going to be between the quick-side guard and the center. And our tight end will bump the man on him and block to the outside.

Let us go back to the five-hole double team between the tight end and the quick-side guard. Say there is a man down in front of the quick-side guard. This is the way we block it: our quick-side guard will come off the football just like he does for the drive block and block the guy with his left shoulder. He will hit and slide his head on the other side. Our tight end will take a step straight down toward the guy he is going to block, and he will block his man right at the waist level. He will block him with his right shoulder and have his head on the outside. The minute the quick-side guard feels the block of that tight end coming down, he swings his hips out, and he and the tight end press their hips together and drive both feet below and move the guy to the inside. You get lateral openings with this type of blocking.

When you just go out and drive block him straight up and then come in and drive block him straight up, if you do not feel those hips, he will split you *every time*! But he cannot split you with our drive-turn block. It is not nearly that complicated. You just have to work on it.

Let us move across the line. Suppose that they have a nose guard on the center and a man lined up on our tight end. There is nobody in front of the quick-side guard, and we call a five-hole play. Our center will snap the ball perfectly and get in position to stop the nose guard from running over you, and the center quick-side guard will come down hard at that belt level. The center will seal his hips, and we get a drive turn with a center quick-side guard. It is all in the five hole. It depends whether the five hole is an odd hole with a man on the center or if the five hole is an even hole, which means there is nobody in front of the center. Those people have to work on their blocks.

We have been very fortunate in the last few years to have a quick-side coach and a strong-side coach. Our quick-side guard takes that tight end and that quick guard, and he works that drive block, that cut-off block, on the right and left side. He also works that drive turn. Then he gets the center and the quick-side guard, and he works on it on the drive turn.

On the strong side, we start out with the center stopping the charge of the nose guard, and the strong guard coming down at belt level. The center swings his hips. Whoever seals the hole is the one who blocks the guy straight up. The guy you are sealing your hips with is the man doing the turn part of the block. So we drive turn on the strong side with the center and the strong guard. Our strong-side line coach will then drive turn with the strong-side guard and the inside tackle. Then he will drive with the inside tackle and the outside tackle. And he also will drive-turn block with the outside tackle and our wingback. We cover double teaming (drive-turn), cut-off, and drive blocking for all linemen. Our quick-side line coach can tell me where they are lining up, and our strong-side line coach can tell me exactly how people are lining up on his side.

Let us close this chapter on line play. I realize we have gone over it very quickly. If you have caught on, it is really simple. Once you *see* it done, you will see that it *is* simple. But it is something you have to work on every week that you work on offense. Every day that we work on offense, we have to do the drive block, we have to do the cut-off block, and we have to do the drive-turn block. Each line coach takes his people. Sometimes they work together; sometimes they do not. They put those blocks together in those groups. These are three blocks we *must* learn: the drive block, the drive-turn, and the cut-off block.

Pulling

One thing that *every* lineman has to learn (except the tight end) is to pull. Our line coaches always work this when the tight end is down with the pass receiver working on pass offense. Every lineman we have has to learn to pull. Our tight end never pulls. He will step down and block the gap inside sometimes. Our quick-side guard pulls to the strong side only. He pulls to the strong side on our sweep. He pulls to the strong side in all but one of the six-hole plays, through the four-hole plays. Our center has to learn to pull to the quick side; he *never* pulls to the strong side. He works on snapping the ball and pulling. There is a technique to pulling, which is described later. Our strong-side guard pulls both ways. He has to pull to the right on the sweep; he has to pull to the left on all the five-hole plays and seven-hole plays. Our inside tackle pulls very little, but we do want him to pull sometimes to the quick side. So we teach him to pull to the quick side. Our outside tackle is the man who leads our reverses. He is the guy that is going to come around that corner on the seven hole, or come up through that five hole, and block the first guy who is not wearing one of our suits. And the wingback will be right behind him running with the football!

In the basic fundamentals of pulling, all linemen who pull use the same technique. Let us say we are teaching all the linemen. The tight end is gone with the backs; they are not there. We are teaching all linemen to pull to the right. I know you think the center does not pull to the strong side, but if we are in left formation, that would be on the quick side. We teach everybody to pull to the right. We want that lineman to go down in a perfect three-point stance, balanced, with forearms resting on his thighs. When the quarterback says, "Set," the lineman's right hand goes down. Our snap count is right after that. The lineman goes on the second word after "Set." When the quarterback says, "Down. Hut," the lineman goes. The quarterback says, "Set. Down. Hut." When the lineman hears that "Hut," he explodes off the ball and runs the play. But when you are pulling to the right and hear that "Hut," you step back and a little bit to the outside with your right foot, and you stay low. You jerk that right arm around, low, as hard as you can, and run all the way around that dummy the coach has out there. He will move that dummy around—a little to the inside, a little to the outside. Everybody has to learn where to go.

When we are pulling left, it is just the opposite. We will say, "Set. Down. Hut." You will quickly step back with your outside foot. Have your eyes down field and run as fast as you can.

We have to have people that can run in our offense. If you are 6'6" and weigh 275 or 280 pounds, you cannot run from here to the field house before dark without help. I don't care how big you are or how strong you are, you *have* to be able to run to play this offense. Some of the great teams ran it in the old days, and it is hard for me to believe this, but The University of Tennessee, which was the single-wing power would not give a scholarship to anybody that weighed over 215 pounds. They said at one time on their offensive line, they had six fullbacks that had played fullback in high school. They were strong and quick and could run. And with this offense, you *have* to run. I do not care how pretty you pull or how you do it, if you cannot get out in front of the ball and throw blocks, you are in trouble. So we really work on pulling every day. You drive block them every day. You cut off. You drive turn. You work on pulling before you start running plays against the defense of the people who are going to play against you that week.

One last thing. We have not emphasized this enough yet, but we will. You cannot play offensive football in an offense like ours with a sloppy, awkward, funny-looking, staggered stance. You line your feet up even. You line them shoulder width apart. You get down in the pre-set position, and you are set right quick. Make sure you spot inside where you think the inside lineman is going to put his hand down, so you can put yours down even with it when you line up. When that quarterback, or that guy calling the snap count says, "Set," you are like that. When he says, "Down. Hut," we are going on that "Hut," and we *have* to explode out of there.

You have to know what your assignment is and where you are going. You cannot get out or pull out of a poor stance. You cannot drive block out of a poor stance. You cannot cut-off block out of one. And you cannot drive turn out of one. I do not know a block you can make in football if you have a poor stance.

If I had my six linemen up there who were 6'6" and all weighed 300 pounds and ran the 40-yard dash in 4'5", I *still* would demand that they get down in a good stance and do their job so they can handle it.

We have purposely left one position out here. We have not discussed the method of playing center in single-wing football. We have already mentioned that people always say, "I don't want to do that; I'm afraid I wouldn't have a center." If you can coach, you can have a center. You cannot only have one, you can have two. And you had better have two and another one training to be that way. We will put down the center's stance and how we teach him to snap the ball when we get started on our offense in our section on the series and will go over it then.

We have briefly gone through line play. We have hurried through it. But if you could take the things that you see here and feel that you can teach them, you can run the single-wing offense. I have never known anybody who wanted to run it that could not run it. I have known some people who talk about it, but they were not willing to study and learn. I know that whatever offense you are running now, you like it the best of all, because you have studied it and you learned it and you know it. And that is exactly what all of us should be doing.

Chapter 6

Backfield Play in the Single-Wing Offense

Personnel: Summary

Tailback (TB)

- He lines up directly behind the center, four yards deep.

- He uses a balanced two-point stance with forearms resting on his thighs.

- He has hands open to take the snap.

- He uses a low stance, easy to start from.

- *He always looks at the football.* We will always have both our TB and FB look at the ball, so the LB's will not know which one is getting the snap.

Fullback (FB)

- He lines up directly behind the strong-side guard.

- He will either be even with the TB or be in a heel-toe relationship with the TB.

- He uses the same stance as the TB.

- He will be low and relaxed.

- *He always looks at the football.* We will always have both our TB and FB look at the ball, so the LB's will not know which one is getting the snap.

Blocking Back

- He lines up in the gap between the SG and the inside tackle.

- He should be 12 to 18 inches deep.

- He takes a balanced three-point stance.

- He calls our snap count, "Set. Down. Hut."

Wingback

- He lines up two feet outside the OT.

- He also lines up two feet deep in the backfield.

- He takes a balanced three-point stance.

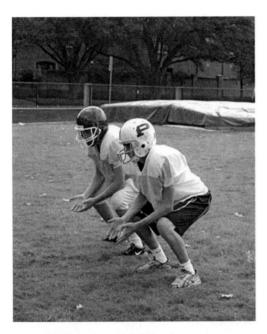

Blocking back and wingback balanced three-point stance

Tailback and fullback stance

Personnel: Alignment

We line up our backfield completely differently than all the football teams we play. Some people get close to lining up our way but not completely.

We have a man in our backfield called the *tailback*. Some people call him the quarterback, because he has to have quarterback ability. The man who plays our tailback will line up directly behind the center four yards deep.

The next man in our backfield is our *fullback*. He will line up directly behind the strong-side guard and four yards deep in the backfield. He will be almost right beside our tailback. Sometimes we let him move up where his heels are even with the tailback's toes. That way, they can move around according to what we are doing on certain plays.

Both the tailback and the fullback have similar jobs. You cannot play any position in our offense unless you can block. A lot of people do not want their quarterback blocking; we have them *all* blocking.

The third backfield man that we line up is unique; no one else has one. When I say that, what I mean is that no one has a blocking back, period. They use some backs to block; but we give him the title *blocking back*. He is very important to our offense. He lines up in the gap. He has his hand down in his stance, just a little behind the strong-side guard and the inside tackle's feet. He is in that gap. Some people call our blocking back a quarterback. He calls our snap count. He does not call plays in the huddle, but he does call our snap count. We depend on him to have a rhythm for that.

We have one more man in the backfield, a *wingback*. He lines up two feet back on the outside tackle and two feet outside the outside tackle. The stance of the tailback and the fullback is different from that of the blocking back and the wingback.

That is how we line up our backfield. When we go left formation, they line up in the same positions but on the other side. We do not number our backs in the sing-wing offense, because it would be very confusing. We have series numbers, and we have names for plays we run. This is a simple method that helps our center in determining his snaps.

When I first started running the single wing, I was told, "How are you going to find the guy every year that is the best runner you have and the best passer?" I probably found that guy three times out of the twenty years that I ran the single wing. So we had to make a decision about what we would do in the case of injury, because we did not want to have to put in someone who was not quite ready to play yet. We start with the tailback.

Tailback

We need the man who is the best runner on our football team at tailback. We like him to be the fastest and the best and the biggest. You do not get that very often. In the forty-three years that I coached and in the twenty years I coached the single wing, I never, not one time, had a running back who weighed two hundred pounds. Everybody in my district had one. I do not know why. Everybody in my district seemed to have one or two, but we never had one. The biggest fullback we ever had weighed a hundred and eighty-five; maybe one weighed one ninety. We just never had big backs. But we need a tailback who is durable. We do not need a dancer back there who dances around. We need someone who can take that football and run north and south and can run our sweep and knows how to follow blocking. Besides that, he has to be able to throw our running pass. We do not do much cup pass, because I never had a tall fullback. We run all of our pass plays off the Teen Series, Ninety Series, and Eighty Series. We have play passes, but our quarterback has to throw. (See chapter on passing.)

Fullback

In our fullback position, we have to have a kid who is pretty tough, someone who can block, someone who has good hands and can catch the snap without any fumbles, and someone who is athletic enough to run our fullback spinner series. Our fullback is not just a blocker. Our fullback has to block, but he is going to carry that football to the strong side. He has to carry that football up the middle. And he has to carry the football to the quick side. We need a good runner who is tough. We do not have to have a big runner, but we need a good runner. We need the best runners we can find, or we will take two good runners and a kid that can run a little bit who can pass. We would like for one of those three people to be a good passer. But he has to play back there and block, and he has to play back there and run. I would like for all of them to be that, but you do not find that in high schools, not in the small high schools like those where I have coached. If we can find three people who can play those two spots back there — tailback and fullback — and work them every day, then if someone gets hurt, we can go right along and function. And we have young kids coming behind them who learn the same thing. Our tailback and our fullback are very, very similar.

Blocking Back

Someone used to call the blocking back the "glorified guard." He does not run the football, but he is the *most important man* in our offense. He is the man who leads our plays, most of the time. We have key breakers, that if you follow him, you have made a bad mistake! But he is the key to our offense. The blocking back in the single-wing offense will always give us the advantage of having one more blocker at the point of attack than the defensive people have. I know defensive people move around and slide around, but we will still have that extra blocker, and we will have our linemen blocking in front of it. Our guards are always pulling to block in front of the ball, and we will have that blocking back blocking too. He calls our snap count, and he is the guy we have to have to get the job done. He thinks he is just a guard playing in the backfield, but he is the *key* to our offense.

The blocking back will line up in the gap between the strong-side guard and the inside tackle. He will be back about two feet. His hand, when it goes down, should be at the same depth as the feet of the strong-side guard and the inside tackle. He cannot crowd up in the line or have his head stuck in the line. We want him right in that gap.

Wingback

Wingbacks are the hardest people to find. The wingback lines up two feet outside and two feet back from the outside tackle. Our wingback has to be a blocker; he has to be a receiver; and he has to be fast enough to run our reverses. Wingbacks are hard to find. We have never used one wingback. I say "never," but sometimes we did not have really but one. We try to play three wingbacks. We want one that we know can block well. We want one that we know can catch the football if we throw it to him. And we want one that we know can run those inside and outside reverses and move the football down the field. So sometimes it takes three wingbacks, and we sub them in and out each play. A lot of times we send plays in with them or the split end. We are still outdated, I know, but we still huddle. We do not signal in plays. Sometimes, we do, but we try to send them in with wingbacks or split ends.

When I first started coaching, I saw the good things that UCLA did under Red Sanders and what Tommy Prothro did when he was at Oregon State. I watched other schools' players who took the stance we do now, and I found out that when you put those people up like that, it is easier for the linebacker to see whom the ball was snapped to. But if you put them down *low* like we have ours and snap the ball back, that linebacker has a difficult time trying to determine which one got the snap. It is hard to key it like that. That is the reason we put them in that position—so it is hard for the linebackers to see who gets the ball.

Overview of Series

Teen Series

This is our Tailback Series to the Strong Side. Our center will use a lead snap to the tailback in all Teen Series plays. We can throw our running pass from this series.

Forty Series

This is our Tailback Series to the Quick Side. Our center will use a direct snap to the tailback in this series. We can throw our quick-side running pass from this series.

Ninety Series

This is our Fullback-Spinner Series. This is the finest series in all of football! Our center will snap the ball directly to the fullback in this series. Our fullback will spin to the tailback. We can hit all points along the line of scrimmage from this series. We can also throw our spin pass to the strong side.

Thirty Series

This is our Direct-Fullback Series. Our center will snap the ball directly to the fullback. He will use a soft snap because our fullback is stepping in to meet the ball. We can run our wedge play, fullback dive, and five-hole cutback.

<u>Note</u>: Some of our plays are given names instead of numbers. We place them in the series that best fits their use.

Chapter 7

Teen Series: Tailback Series to Strong Side

The Teen Series has four plays—*Sweep*, *16*, *Blast*, and *15 Reverse*.

Sweep

The first play we would teach in our Teen Series would be the *Sweep*. The *18 Pass Play* is in that series, but we include it in the pass offense (See Chapter 11). The first play we teach is the Sweep. See diagram. We have it blocked against every conceivable defense that we have looked at before. It is the thing we are going to hang our hat on! It is the one we *have* to run to make our offense go.

16

Our next play in the Teen Series is *16*. If you are going to play wide and stop our sweep, our *Off-Tackle Play 16* is going to hurt your defense. These are the things we set up. This play has been very, very consistent and very good for us. On 16 we get a drive-turn block with the wingback and outside tackle. We get a block out on the man coming across the line of scrimmage—the forced guy—with our blocking back. We pull the quick-side guard through the hole, sealed to the inside, and the fullback takes two steps to the outside, and he goes through the hole and blocks the outside of it. Our tailback takes three steps and plants his right foot and hits straight up field, north and south.

Blast

The next play in our Teen Series is the other hang-your-hat play, called the *Blast*. The I-formation people call it the isolation play, and it is an isolation. It isolates the linebacker with two blockers on him. This is a short-yardage play. And it is a long-yardage play. It is one we can run from anywhere on the field. We believe we can make yards on it.

15 Reverse

The last play in our Teen Series is our *15 Reverse*. Our ball will be snapped to the tailback, and he and the fullback will head to the strong side like the Sweep and the 16. When he gives a front handoff to the wingback, coming back in front of him, he hits straight up in the five hole. On the diagram you can see how the double team blocks, and you see the people who pull. On this play we block out with the blocking back. We pull the strong guard and send him to the inside. He seals the hole. And we pull the outside tackle and pull him through the hole to the outside. This has been a very, very good misdirection play for us through the years. This completes the Teen Series.

"Sweep"

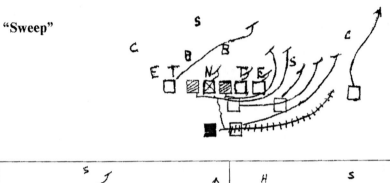

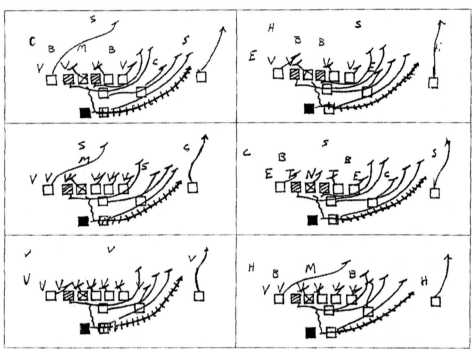

TE	Block across.	TB	Take lead snap and run the Sweep.
QG	Pull and lead Sweep.	FB	Sprint the strong side and block the first man to show.
C	Block on or backside.		
SG	Pull and seal on LB. If loaded, cutoff on man on.	BB	Sprint the strong side and block the first man to show.
IT	Block man on or man over SG.	WB	Cutoff on the contain man.
OT	Cutoff block on man over you.		
SE	Block outside 1/3.		

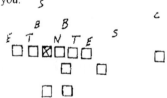

"16"

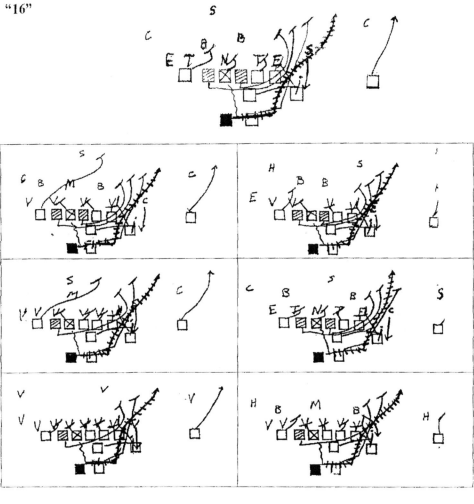

TE	Block inside or down field	TB	Take lead snap and take three steps to the strong side. Cut up 6-hole.
QG	Pull and seal 6-hole		
C	Block on or backside.	FB	Start toward strong side and cut up the 6-hole. Block first man to show.
SG	Pull and seal on 6-hole. If loaded, block on.		
		BB	Block out on contain at 6-hole.
IT	Block on or man over SG.	WB	D/T with OT on man over him.
OT	D/T with WB on man on.		
SE	Block outside 1/3.		

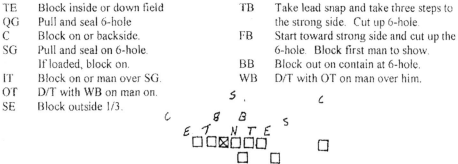

"Blast"

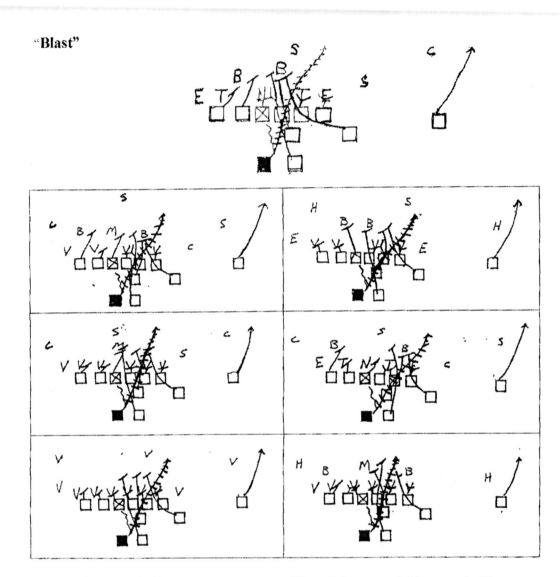

TE	Block on or inside.	**TB**	Take snap and drive over the IT.
QG	Block man on or inside.	**FB**	Block over the IT on LB.
C	(Odd) D/T with SG.	**BB**	Team up with WB and block play side
	(Even) Block on.		LB.
SG	(Odd) D/T with Center.	**WB**	Team up with BB and block play side
	(Even) D/T with IT		LB.
IT	(Odd) Block man on.		
	(Even) D/T with SG.		
OT	Drive block man on.		
SE	Block inside out on deep 1/3.		

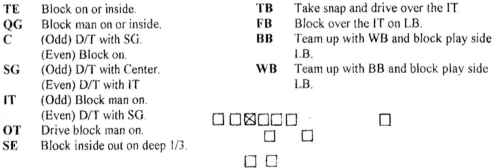

"15 Reverse"

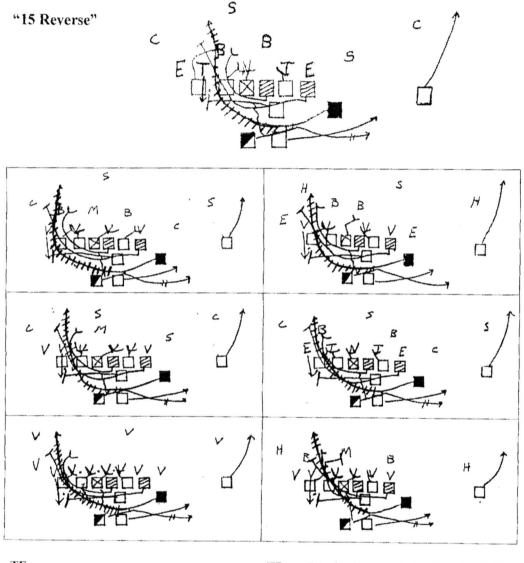

TE	TB	Take lead snap and give front handoff to WB.
QG		
C	FB	Fake wide to strong side.
SG	Block the same as 45 except OT pull	BB	Block out at the 5-hole.
IT	and lead through 5-hole.	WB	Open step to the Quick side and take a
OT			front handoff from TB. Hit the 5-hole.
SE			

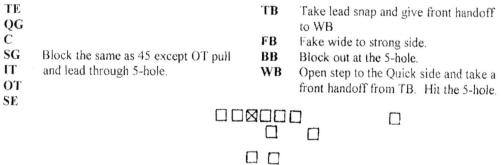

Chapter 8

Forty Series: Tailback Series to Quick Side

The next series we teach is our Forty Series. This is our tailback series that we run to the quick side instead of the strong side. It has three plays—*40 Trap*, *45*, and *Flicker*.

40 Trap

Off of the Forty Series, we run a *40 Trap*, where the tailback makes a half spin and hits up the middle on the trap play, which will be explained with each play. The diagram shows it against all defenses. One of the unique things about this play is that if you run on us with a nose guard, we can trap your nose guard from inside out with our blocking back. We think this is the best trap in football!

45

The next play we teach is the bread-and-butter play, and it may as well be a hang-your-hat play to the quick side, because *45* is a power, off-tackle play! On the diagram, you can see a double team with a quick-side-end guard. You can see the fullback and the blocking back kicking out the defensive end. And you can see the strong-side guard inside the hole and the wingback coming through the hole to the outside. 45 is a great play if they decide that they are going to over hit and slide to the strong side. It has been very consistent for us.

Flicker

The last play in the Forty Series is what we call the *Flicker*. We make it look just like *45*. The only difference is that our tailback will take the ball, take a step to his left, pause, and hit right through the five hole. But he will put the ball back on his right hip. (We only run this from the right formation.) The wingback will pick it off coming wide around that side. It is very deceptive. Goodness, I do not know how many two-point conversions we have made or how many times we have broken the long runs on the Flicker Play!

"40 Trap"

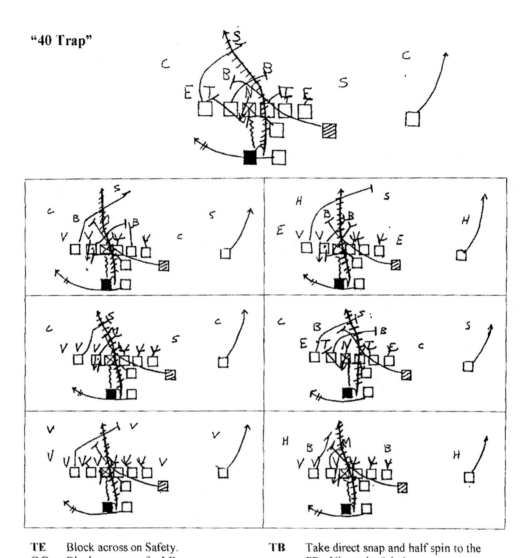

TE	Block across on Safety.	**TB**	Take direct snap and half spin to the
QG	Block across on far LB.		FB. Hit up the 0-hole.
C	(Odd) Pull to quick side and block man	**FB**	Fake behind the TB to the Quick side.
	over QG area..	**BB**	Trap block inside out the first man from
	(Even) D/T with SG.		the Center's nose to the Quick side.
SG	(Odd) D/T with IT.	**WB**	Pull and clean out the 0-hole. Block
	(Even) D/T with Center.		the weak-side LB.
IT	(Odd) DT with SG.		
	(Even) Man on you.		
OT	Block man over you.		
SE	Block deep 1/3.		

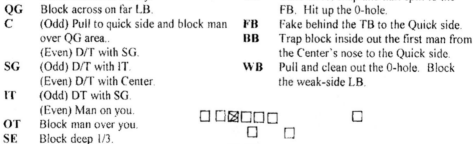

"45"

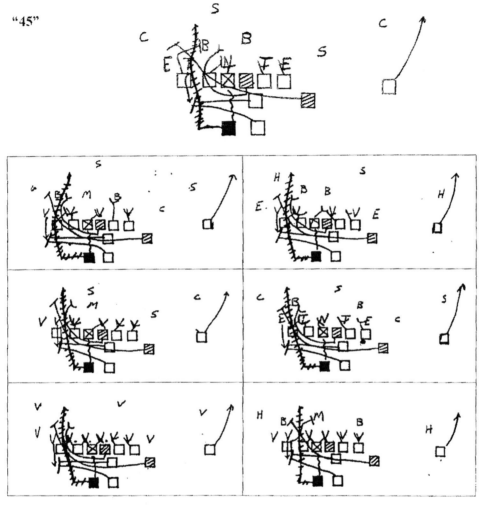

TE	Block inside. D/T with QG on an even defense.
QG	(Odd) D/T with Center on Nose. (Even) D/T with TE.
C	(Odd) D/T with QG on Nose. (Even) Block man over SG.
SG	Pull and seal inside 5-hole.
IT	Block man on or inside.
OT	Block man over you.
SE	Block deep 1/3.

TB	Take direct snap and step to the Quick side. Pause and drive up the 5-hole.
FB	Team up with BB and block out on first man past QG.
BB	Team up with FB and block out on first man past QG.
WB	Pull and lead play through the 5-hole.

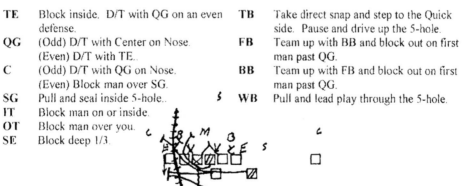

"Flicker"

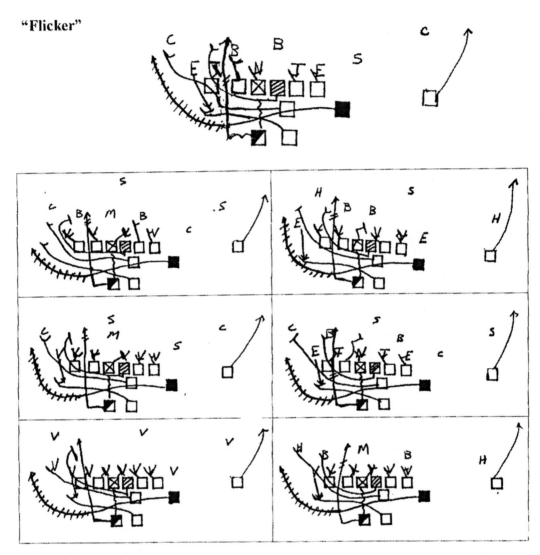

TE Cut off block on man over you or first man outside.	**TB** Take direct snap and step back and to the quick side. Pause and hit into 5-hole. Place ball on your right hip and let WB pick it off.
QG Cut off man over you.	
C Block on or man over SG.	
SG Pull and lead through 7-hole.	**FB** Block to the quick side and hook block the first man to show.
IT Block on or inside.	
OT Block on and then downfield.	**BB** Block to the quick side and dip inside the FB's block and block the HB.
SE Block middle 1/3.	
	WB Sprint to the quick side and take the ball off of the TB's hip and swing wide.

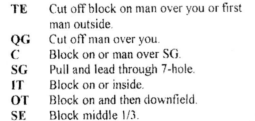

Chapter 9

Thirty Series: Fullback Direct/Quick Series

The next series we teach is our Thirty Series. Some people call this our Fullback-Direct Series. We have three plays in it—the *Dive Play*, the *Wedge*, and the *37 Power*—which are diagrammed with blocks against all the defenses that we have seen with it.

Dive Play

The first play we have off of this series is what we call the *Dive Play*. It is nothing but a fullback blast play, but we call it the Dive Play and have always left it that way. You isolate that linebacker. The fullback is coming right up in there. It has been very good for us. The blocking back and the wingback go through the hole and block the linebacker, and the fullback will follow straight ahead with the ball. The tailback will either stand up and fake a pass or sweep out to the right. That is our Dive Play. We could call it the Fullback Dive, and sometimes we probably do. But this is the only Dive Play we have.

Wedge

The next play is the *Wedge Play*. The Wedge is a hundred years old. We wedge the man in front of our center. We will run it on the goal line. We will run it on first down. We will even throw off of it. We will run it and jump and let our back jump and hit our tight end with a jump pass. The Wedge is this: if they have a nose guard on our center, all our offensive linemen will seal down inside, and every one of them will try to get a shoulder pad on that nose guard. If you are realistic and if you can picture that, you know it never happens.

Our center and our quick-side guard and our strong guard are going to, all three, hit that nose guard and stop him or drive him. And then the inside and outside tackle are going to come down and join in the pile and push. The blocking back blocks to the quick side, right over where the tight end lined up to pick up anybody coming inside. Our wingback comes down inside and blocks anybody coming over the outside tackle. Our tailback, once again, fakes a pass or fakes to the sweep. Our fullback gets the ball and runs. We teach him to dive on the goal line. We do that by using a stand-up dummy. We let him dive in the pole-vault pit or the high-jump pit, where he cannot get hurt. We lay dummies down and put one where he learns to dive over it and land on the dummies, so he does not get hurt. The Wedge has been a great goal-line play for us. It is also a great play to come up and run the jump pass from.

If there is not a man in front of our center, we wedge the man in front of our strong guard. Every offensive lineman except the split end, who is out too wide, is sealed toward the middle, and we all try to wedge the same man. What that does is tighten up the gaps, and nobody can get through, so we run our fullback in there.

The Wedge is the only play we run in our offense that we go on "Set." Every play we run has the snap count, "Set. Down. Hut." And we go on the "Hut." We get in a rhythm. When we are in the pre-set position and run the Wedge the defense is surprised. We never fail to make yardage. But we have to seal each other well, so they cannot split us in between.

37 Power

The last play on the Thirty Series is our *37 Power*. This is our fullback sweep to the weak side. In the diagram you can see the blocking and the people that we get out in front of the football when people over shift on us. This is the only play when the center might get a little confused. He needs to get the ball to our fullback, right straight at him, just like he does on the Dive Play, but be sure he gets there quickly. This is really our fullback sweep to the quick side. The tight end will hook the man on him. The quick guard will hook the man on him. The center will block the nose guard or block back away from the play. The strong guard will pull and lead it. The blocking back goes and leads it. The tailback goes and leads it also. The fullback follows those blockers around the left side. People who over shift on us will get hurt badly with the wide reverses, and they will get hurt by the fullback 37 Power, which gives us a great sweep to get our fullback to the quick side. If you notice, our fullback does not just run inside. He runs to the strong side. He is going to run up the middle. You will see in the Ninety Series, he is going to run wide. We are going to use him all over their defense!

"Dive"

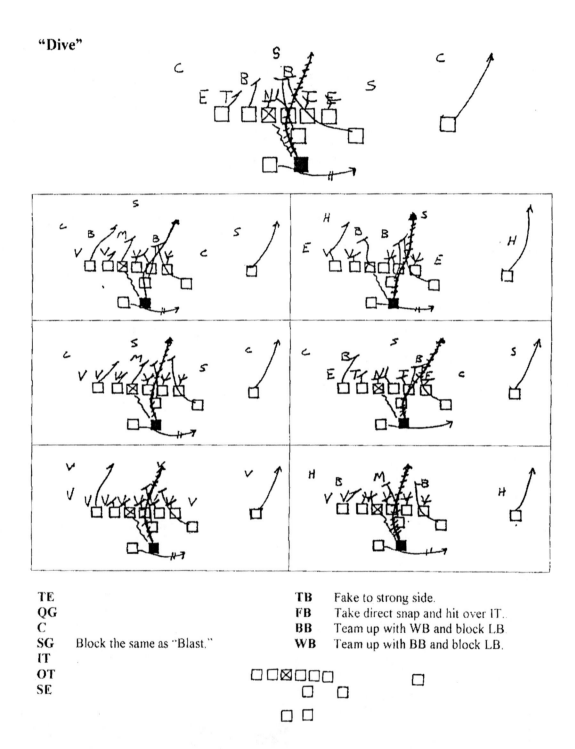

TE		**TB**	Fake to strong side.
QG		**FB**	Take direct snap and hit over IT.
C		**BB**	Team up with WB and block LB.
SG	Block the same as "Blast."	**WB**	Team up with BB and block LB.
IT			
OT			
SE			

"Wedge"

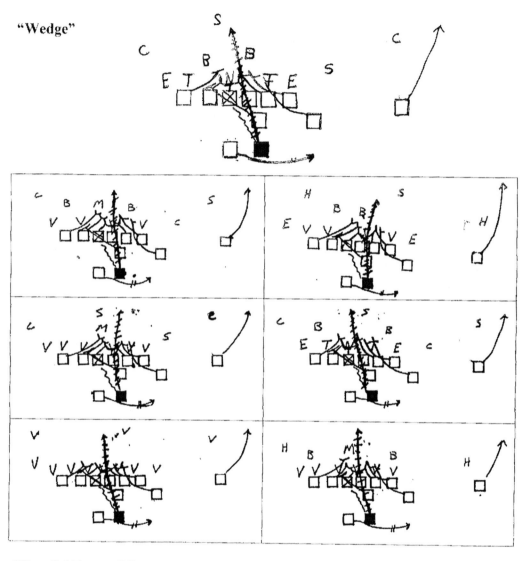

TE	Fold in over QG.	**TB**	Fake to the strong side.
QG	Fold in over Center.	**FB**	Take direct snap and hit over the Apex of the Wedge. Dive on short yardage.
C	(Odd) Apex for Wedge. (Even) Wedge with SG.	**BB**	Block to the quick side. Fill spot over the Center's left leg.
SG	(Odd) Wedge with Center.		
IT	Fold in over SG.	**WB**	Fold in over the inside leg of the IT.
OT	Fold in over IT.		
SE	Block deep 1/3		

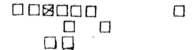

"37 Power"

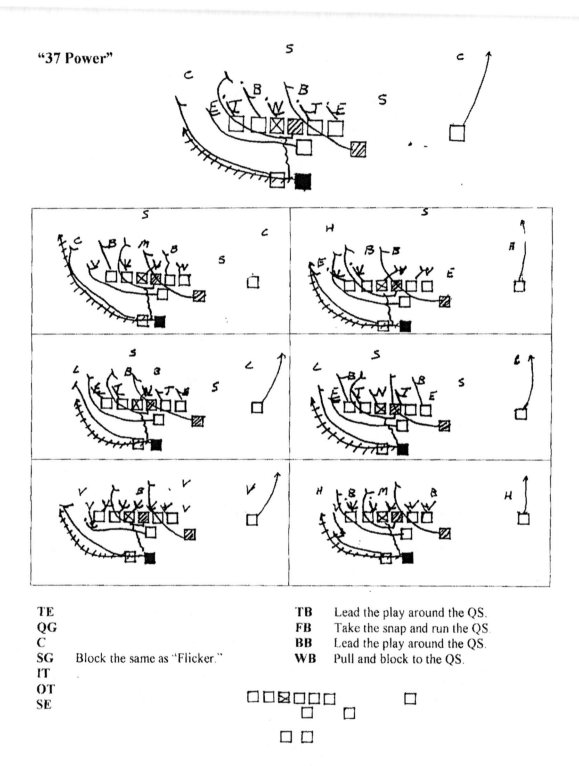

TE		**TB**	Lead the play around the QS.
QG		**FB**	Take the snap and run the QS.
C		**BB**	Lead the play around the QS.
SG	Block the same as "Flicker."	**WB**	Pull and block to the QS.
IT			
OT			
SE			

Chapter 10

Ninety Series: Fullback Spinner Series (Best in All Football!)

The last series is the one, as I have stated before, that we think is the most deceptive series in football. Without it I am not sure how we could run the single wing. The first years we coached the single wing, we ran the Draw Series like they run it on the spread. But about four years into it, we went to the Spinner Series, and that made a *huge* difference. We run five plays off of our Ninety Series — *96, 94, 90 Trap, 95 Reverse*, and *97 Reverse*.

96

In our Ninety Series, the first play we put in is the *96*. We have a 98 Pass, but that goes in the pass offense. In 96, our linemen block exactly like they did on 16. The only difference is that we snap the ball to the fullback who runs a fullback spinner, hands the ball to the tailback who hits through the six hole, and the fullback fakes up the middle. I will go over the fullback spin in detail later.

94

The next play is an off-tackle play inside called *94*. This is our fullback's great running play that we run over and over. The ball goes to the fullback. He spins. He does not fake to anybody.

The tailback fakes like he is going wide to the strong side. The fullback will spin and hit the four hole. We pull the quick-side guard to block through the four hole. The blocking back will block out on the man over our outside tackle. It has been a great running play for our fullback.

90 Trap

The next play our fullback runs in our Ninety Series is the *90 Trap*. It has the same blocking as our 40 Trap does for our linemen and the rest of the backs. The only thing is the tailback does not get to snap. The fullback gets it, spins, and hits straight up over where the center lined up. Our tailback will fake to the right. This has been a great trap for us. We have had many long, long runs off of it.

95 Reverse

The next play is one of our misdirection plays off the Ninety Series—the *95 Reverse*. It is blocked the same as 15 Reverse. It is a five-hole misdirection play. The fullback takes the ball and spins. The tailback fakes to the strong side. The wingback comes *behind* the fullback, takes the hand-off, and hits up the five-hole.

97 Reverse

The last play we put in the Ninety Series is the *97 Reverse*. Same thing. The fullback takes the snap, spins, and hands the ball to the wingback coming around behind him. The fullback fakes up the middle. The tailback fakes the strong side. We run this play *wide*. This is like the way we run our 37, our hook-sweep play. We try to hook the outside man, cut off with our tight end, and cut off with our guard. We make sure to get the blocking back, the tailback, and the strong guard out front blocking, and we pull the wingback up through the hole if he can get there.

Teaching the Fullback to Spin

This section is on teaching the Spinner Series to our fullback—our Ninety Series. There are several different ways you can spin on the Ninety Series. The one we picked up and like the most and is the one I think is the most consistent is the one I will explain now.

To be consistent with the Spinner Series we discovered that there was only one way we thought we could really teach it. When we first decided to put this in, there were several colleges still running the single wing across the country. I got in touch with Oregon State University. Tommy Prothro had coached there and taken them to the Rose Bowl running the single wing. He sent me a letter telling me how they taught the fullback to spin. Our coaching staff looked at the letter, and we looked at each other and thought that this was a pretty good way to do it, we guessed. We got a couple of other colleges to send us film. They were teaching the spinner differently. We picked up the way Wichita Falls High School and Wichita Falls Rider High School in Texas were teaching their spinner. We settled on the one that Oregon State had, because it was very similar to the one Wichita Falls and Wichita Falls Rider did.

This is the way we think we have to teach it. The first thing we do is to take the two or three backs that we know we will use in the spinner position. They can also play the tailback spot or the spinner back spot, which is the fullback. We try to take three people that we teach how to spin on this.

We put those three people whom we have chosen as our spinner backs in the stance we use—the crouch stance with their forearms resting on their thighs and their hands open. We discovered very quickly the worst thing you can do is take a center and a football with those backs and try to teach them to spin that way. We do not even have the center *look* at a football until he has learned those three steps we have to have. The way we teach it is from that stance.

The first thing you do when the ball is snapped is to take a short, six-to-eight inch step right out in the middle of your stance (where the middle of your stance was). And when you step there, you drop your rear down and have your back straight. We call those two things *step, drop*. We repeat it over and over. We do not want a fast spinner; we do not want a slow spinner. We want a rhythmic spin. We want to have it the same every time. *Step, drop, spin. Step, drop, spin* is the way we teach it. But we teach it one part at a time.

The first thing we do when we say the snap count is to take that short, six-to-eight inch step right out in the middle of their stance and drop their tail. We will say, "Step, drop." We go back to our stance again and say, "Step, drop." We go back to our stance *again* and say, "Step, drop." We repeat it several times. Then we add the second part. "Step, drop." "Step, drop." We put the *drop* in. Sometimes we have found it easier to teach them the *step, drop* together rather than the *step* then the *drop*. You can do it either way. But the main thing is that you not let the fullback or spinner back have a football and that you not let him wonder whom he hands it to or whom he fakes to. Do not let him do anything like that. Just make sure he learns how to step and drop with his right foot six-to-eight inches right out in the middle of his stance.

Once we get the step and the drop down, keeping their backs straight, then we stop and go back to the stance again and talk about the spin itself. Once again, before I get to the spin itself, you are not going to spin well, not the way we are teaching it, until you can do the step and drop in a *rhythm*. Step, drop, with your back straight. Why do we want your back straight? Because if it is not straight, when you spin, you will spin all over that backfield, and you will not have control of your body.

The third part of our step, drop is the *spin* part. We say, "Step, drop," taking that short six-to-eight inch step right in the middle of your stance. You drop your rear end down, and your back is straight. And then we say, "Spin."

We spin in a *counter-clockwise* motion. We are spinning off of our right foot that we took the step with. All the weight should be on it. It is hard to do in slow motion. You have to have the rhythm—step, drop, spin. Once we add the spin to the step-drop, it is very smooth and easy to do. Your back is straight. You have your body in perfect control.

When you spin, you spin counter-clockwise, all the way around. You are on your right foot only. You pick up your left foot and bring it around. You should come out of your spin with your left foot pointed right where our inside left tackle lines up. We put a cone there or something to show our spinner backs where their foot should be pointed when they come out. So you do step, drop, spin. We do not go any further than that. Just step, drop, spin and stay right there.

Let us talk about it again. I realize this is complicated just looking at it on a piece of paper. Just go out and do it. You cannot go out and put it all in right now. First of all, it has to be stance. Then step, drop. Step, drop. Now when the spin gets there, and you spin counter-clockwise, you come out with your left foot up, bringing it around and pointing it right where our inside tackle lines up.

After you step, drop, and spin around with your left foot pointed where the inside tackle lines up, you have to remember this: while you are spinning *stay low*. Stay down low. There is no use spinning and standing up and coming around. It is easy for them to see you that way. The drop is put in there to keep your back straight and keep you low, so they cannot see you.

After we get our backs to do that, we go out each day and take a few minutes and work them—individually or all three together. Step, drop, spin. Step, drop, spin.

The next thing we do is to give each of the spinner backs a football. Put it in his hands and tell him, "Now we are going to do the step, drop, spin." What he is thinking about is, "What do I do with the football?" Let me make this really plain. We never fake the ball to anybody in the Spinner Series. There is no use holding the ball out and showing it to the defense when we are spinning around. Our fullback, or spinner back as we call him, will take the football and put it in his stomach with both hands, with his arms over it and spin that way. When he comes out, it is hard for the defense to see him, and he is down low. Did he keep the ball, did he give the ball, or what? The back whom he is handing it to or faking it to does all the faking. He just spins, and that back does the fake. On our *96*, he will hand it off to the tail back, which we will discuss later. He spins and keeps the ball close to himself.

To review, we give each of them a football. There is no center yet. We are not ready for that. Simply step, drop, spin. After we get it pretty smooth, then we let each one of them go, one at a time. They have a cone out there that they are to be pointed toward when they come out with that left foot. Then it is step, drop, spin, and *run*. He comes out this time, and when he comes out with that foot pointed toward where the inside tackle lines up, he just runs right over the top of that corner, to the right or left of it. That is the rhythm he is going to use and that is the way he is going to run it on *every* play. There is one exception to that. As you know, there is always an exception. When we run the *90 Trap*, he brings the leg around and points it up, as close as he can, to the strong-side guard stance, but we will get to that later. One more time—step, drop, spin, run. Step, drop, spin, and run.

Then we add the center to it. He has to concentrate on getting the snap and putting the ball in his pocket. Step, drop, spin, and run. The play he runs is *94*. That's a great running play for our fullback. He has run many, many, many yards off of that play—the *94*. We are going to run it a bunch of times in the game.

If you put the center in at first, the fullback will be concentrating on catching the ball. So we wait until he learns the step, drop, spin, and run before we add the center. They said "Step, drop, spin, and run" in their minds a lot, but after a while, they let it go. They will forget it and just do it automatically. One thing we learned the hard way. You think you have it taught, and you practice it every day, and you look up one day, and there is an extra step in there somewhere, or he is stepping too far with his right foot, or he is not stepping far enough. He is dropping his rear and is trying to straighten his back some, but he is not keeping the stance low when he spins. You have to concentrate on it *constantly*. We tell them to work on it at home, but sometimes they make more bad habits that way. They will get it down. Once you get it down, it is a powerful, powerful help to the offense. Without the Fullback Spinner Series (Ninety Series), I do not think we would have ever stayed with the single wing long at all.

We have it all now. We think we have it. We have the step, the drop, the spin, and the run. Now we come to the two other things the fullback has to learn. He learns quickly that when he hears "Ninety Series," he keeps the ball on the *94* and *90 Trap*. But also in the Ninety Series are the *98 Pass*, *96*, *95 Reverse*, and *97 Reverse* plays.

On *96* he knows he is going to hand the ball to the tailback. Which hand does he use? You are either going to hand it to the tailback or the wingback. If you hand it to the tailback, you hand it with your left hand—the hand closest to the tailback when lined up. You will hand it to the tailback when you are facing away from the line of scrimmage. But you do not stop your spin. You make one continuous step, drop, spin. The spin and the handoff take place at the same time. If you hand it to the wingback, you hand it to him with your right hand—the hand closest to him when you lined up for the play. You spin around, put the ball out, and he takes it.

The way the tailback and wingback take the football is up to them. We used to have them put it in the pocket, but they bumped into too many elbows. Then we had them take it in their hand, but they did not get a good hand. But we run it until they get it smooth. We want whatever is comfortable for them. I personally like for them to take it in their hands.

To review the Spinner Series, we teach three backs and line up to teach the stance first. Then teach the step, drop, spin. They do not run yet. Then we give each one of them a football. They step, drop, spin counterclockwise, bringing the left leg around pointing where the inside tackle lined up, with back straight, staying low, and then run. The next thing we add is the center to get the snap right.

When we get ready to run *98 Pass* or *96*, we have a tailback with them, and hand the ball off to the tailback and continue running. Then we will put a wingback with our spinner back, and we will run the step, drop, spin. The fullback will give him the ball with his right hand. When we get to the handoff, we find we have one real problem. When the fullback steps, drops, and spins, he starts looking for the back he is going to hand it to, or he will spin around fast to get it to the tailback. But the tailback has to time when he goes with the spinner back's rhythm. And the wingback can come running full speed, because he will get there just about the right time for the handoff. He will be right at the handoff spot behind our fullback when he has spun around and is facing him.

It sounds complicated. It is something you have to work on. They get better and better at it. We have reels and reels of film and DVD's showing that this is exactly how they are spinning. Every now and then, they get an extra step in there, or their back is not straight, or they are not low. You have to go back to fundamentals and work it day after day after day. But I promise you that this series will make your offense explode. In running our single wing with the end over, this did more for our passing game and more for our spinning game (deceptive game) than *anything* we did.

"96"

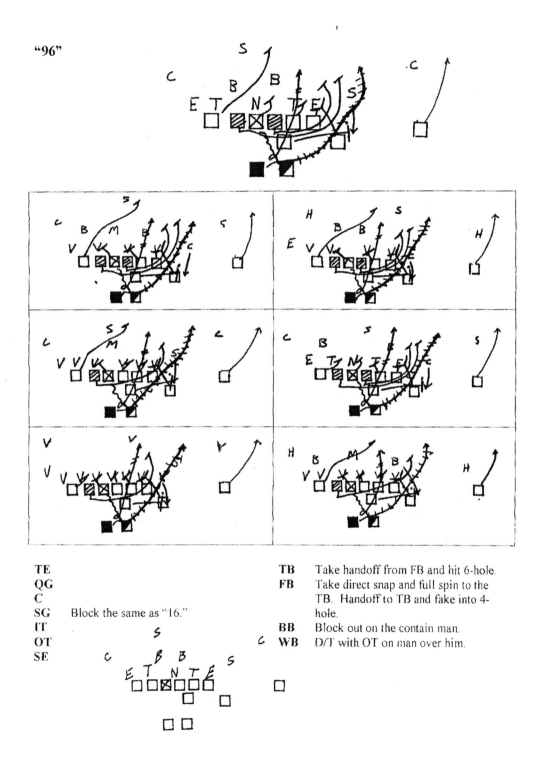

TE		**TB**	Take handoff from FB and hit 6-hole.
QG		**FB**	Take direct snap and full spin to the
C			TB. Handoff to TB and fake into 4-
SG	Block the same as "16."		hole.
IT		**BB**	Block out on the contain man.
OT		**WB**	D/T with OT on man over him.
SE			

85

"94"

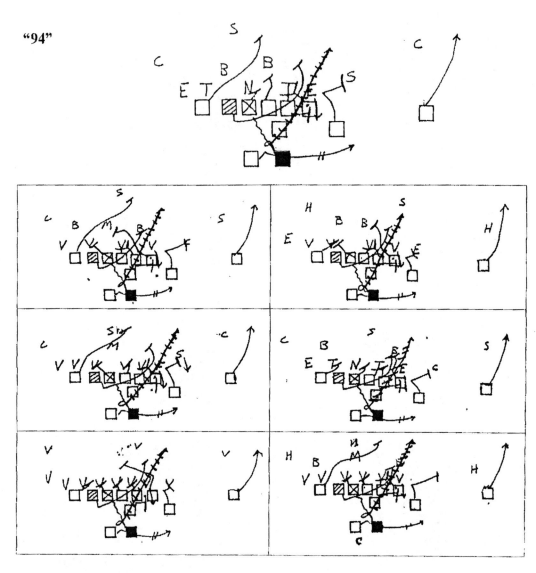

TE	Block across or scoop block inside.	TB	Fake to the strong side.
QG	Pull and lead through 4-hole.	FB	Take direct snap and full spin to TB.
C	Block on or man over QG.		Drive up the 4-hole.
SG	(Odd) Block on or LB.	BB	Block inside out on man over OT.
	(Even) D/T with IT.	WB	Bake block at man over OT and then
IT	(Odd) D/T with OT.		block inside out on contain man.
	(Even) D/T with SG.		
OT	(Odd) D/T with IT		
	(Even) Block down inside on far LB.		
SE	Block inside out on deep 1/3.		

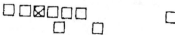

"90 Trap"

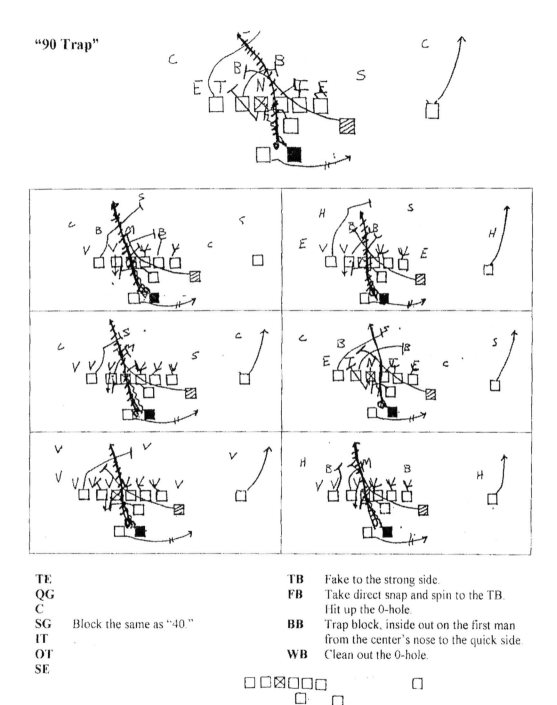

TE		TB	Fake to the strong side.
QG		FB	Take direct snap and spin to the TB.
C			Hit up the 0-hole.
SG	Block the same as "40."	BB	Trap block, inside out on the first man
IT			from the center's nose to the quick side.
OT		WB	Clean out the 0-hole.
SE			

"95 Reverse"

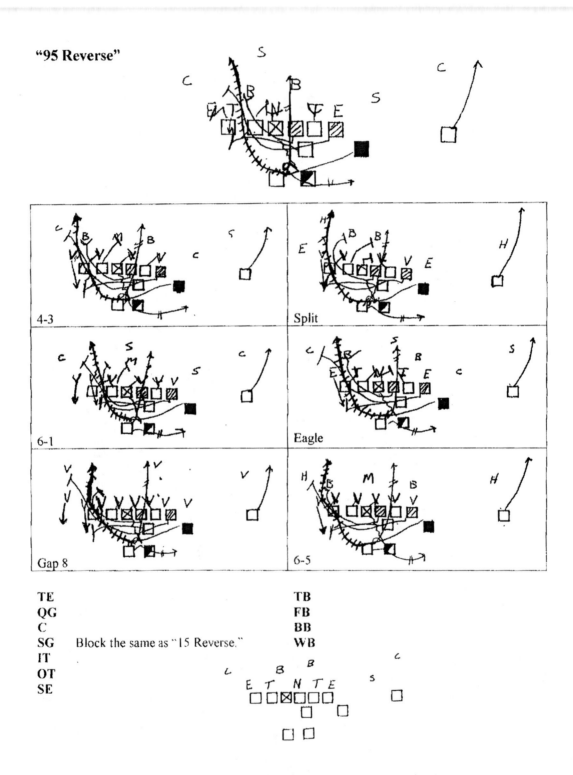

TE		TB
QG		FB
C		BB
SG	Block the same as "15 Reverse."	WB
IT		
OT		
SE		

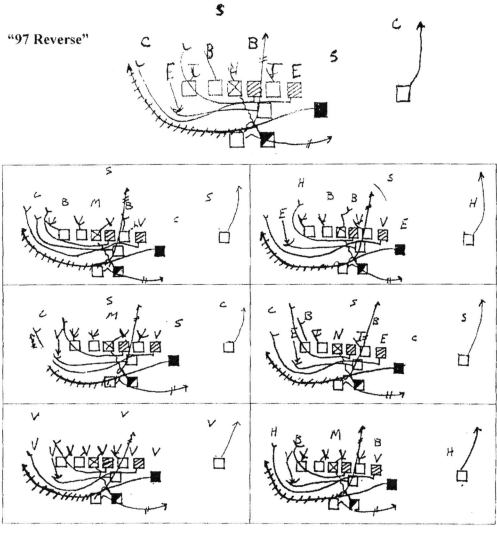

"97 Reverse"

TE	**TB**	Fake to the strong side.
QG	**FB**	Take snap and full spin to the TB.
C	Block the same as "Flicker" except	Hand off to WB coming behind you.
SG	OT will pull and lead the play wide.	Fake into the 4-hole.
IT		**BB**	Lead play around the 7-hole.
OT		**WB**	Sprint behind the FB and take handoff.
SE			Run wide around the 7-hole.

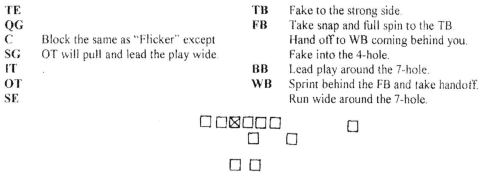

Chapter 11

Pass Offense: The Passing Game

Pass Offense

We have never thrown out of the pocket in the single wing. I say never, but very little have we ever, because we want to throw the football on the run. We want our running pass to look just like our sweep to the strong side. We give letters to describe our receivers. Our split end is X, our tight end is Y, and our wingback is Z. We try to protect our passer, and we felt like it was easier to protect him with a moving cup, like the running pass, than it was to stand up in the pocket. We have never had the 6'4" or 6'5" quarterback who could stand back there and just throw over good defensive people. So we threaten them every time with the run and try to make it look just like our sweep.

To the split end, which is X, we throw the following patterns. We run *18 Pass X Curl*, *18 Pass X Square*, *18 Pass X Deep*, and *18 Pass X Square and Up*. Those are the four routes that he learns to run. Every one of our pass plays off of our 18 Pass Series comes off of the sweep action. It looks like we are running the sweep to the strong side. A lot of people call that the *moving pocket*. We protect the backside of our passer with our blocking back, which is one of the times he goes away from where the play is. That really bothers linebackers if they are keying him.

We throw on the run. We get our junior-high kids started by learning to throw on the run. It is really not that complicated. When we take that snap from center, we put the ball under that right arm and start that wide sweep full speed. After about four steps, we bring that football up with both hands in front of us, looking down field for the pass route we have called. But we must square those shoulders with the line of scrimmage and throw that football right at the target. If I am running the same way the receiver is, you do not have to lead the receiver at all. You throw it right at him. And the ball will be right. If you lead him, you are going to always be too far in front of him.

One of the biggest things we have to work on is making sure our passer, when he is running to his right or to his left, keeps his shoulders squared up. The passer cannot throw across his body on the run, for he would throw the ball behind the receiver (since a football is not spheroid like all other balls). He will never ever be consistent throwing it that way. So he throws that football straight over his shoulder with his shoulders square (parallel to the line of scrimmage).

I would love sometime to have a pocket pass here or there. We do sometimes pull up two steps and throw back to the backside, but we do not think we really have the time to teach all of this. So we are going to make sure we are going to throw on the run. It has been very, very successful for us in the passing game.

Split End/Split Receiver

We try to play three to five split ends. Sometimes we have two or three who could not catch a ball if you ran down there and handed it to them. But remember they have a *very* important job to do in our offense. Every time the ball is snapped, they make an outside release and sprint down that field. If a pass is called, they run a route. If a pass has not been called, they sprint fifteen yards as hard as they can and make that corner back go with them or whomever is covering them. He has to cover our split end. Someone said that even if he did not have any hands, he would have to cover him, because he might nub one with his elbows and catch it for a touchdown. You cannot do that with one split end. When you do that every play, you could not do that with only one receiver. If you do that every play of the game, that corner back gets tired of chasing this guy. After a while, he thinks that they are not going to throw to him at all.

18-Pass Routes

We have letters for our ends and wingbacks. Our split end is X, our tight end is Y, and our wingback is Z. We call the pass route for our receiver. If we run a pass called *18 Pass Z Quick*, immediately our split end knows he goes down and curls to the inside, and our wingback runs a quick route out in the flat.

The next route we run is *18 Pass X Curl*. It is the same pattern as the 18 Pass Z Quick. X will go downfield, curl, and the wingback will run the Z Quick.

We teach the *18 Pass X Square* next. Our end has to drive that corner off, and about ten yards down field he plants his left foot as it hits the ground, then runs a square route to the outside without rounding it off. He might even come back a little.

18 Pass X Deep is the next route we throw off our 18 Pass Series. We run downfield and take him downfield with us, and if he does not cover him, we just run 18 X Deep and throw the ball to the split end deep.

Another play in our regular 18-Pass Routes is the *18 Pass X Squared Up*. X will square out about five yards and break up field. We really hit some good deep touchdown passes off of this route. One might think, "You do not throw it to anybody but the split end." On these, it is either the split end or the wingback. It is only for the Z Quick, the X Curl, the X Square, the X Deep, or X Squared Up.

Sometimes while we are running the 18-Pass Route, our tight end goes down the middle of the field and, after about five yards deep, crosses in a drag route. It is the *18 Pass Y Flag* and is one of the *best* plays we run. We score more two-point conversions on this play than all the rest put together! When we go for two, we are going to throw the flag. In the 18 Pass Y Flag, what does

X do? He runs the curl. What does Z do? He runs the quick. What does Y do? He starts that drag across the middle of the field and cuts back out to the flag (end zone). We also have the *18 Pass Y Drag* (middle) and the *18 Pass Y Deep* (straight out).

In the *X Curl and Pitch* we run the 18 Pass where X will curl, the tailback will throw the ball straight to him, the wingback will come around outside the X, and X will catch the ball and lateral it to the wingback as he goes down the sideline. This has also been a very good play for us.

All of these pass routes are diagrammed on the 18 Pass sheet.

98 Pass

In addition to the 18 Pass Routes, we throw a play call the *98 Pass*, which is off our Fullback Spinner Series. In the 98 Pass there is one route. Our split end will run the deep route down the field. Our wingback will not run the Z Quick but will go down about eight yards and run a square route out behind the split end's deep pattern. And our tight end will drag across the middle deep and take the snap with the fullback, hand it to the tailback, and the fullback will fake up the middle. Our blocking back goes toward the play—the eight hole; he is out to the right to block the outside man to give our tailback a chance to throw the 98 Pass. He can throw it to the wingback, deep split end, to the man across,... to whomever is open.

Play Passes

Play passes are when we take the football and make it look just like a running play. We have made ours look like the Sweep every time so far. But the play passes we have are different. We run a play called the *Blast Pass*. The center will snap the ball to the tailback. He will come right in there on the blast, and just before he hits the line of scrimmage, jump and hit our tight end or a little quick route (or pump route as we call it) right in the open crease.

Next we run the same pattern called the *Dive Pass*. This snap goes to the fullback. He runs in there, jumps, and hits the wingback or the tight end on the little short route. Of the tailback and the fullback, we know that the tailback will probably be the better passer. We want our fullback to be able to throw this on short yardage or down on the goal line.

We have made lots of good plays off the next play pass—the *97 Reverse Pass*. The ball goes to the fullback; he spins counterclockwise and hands the ball to the wingback coming behind him. When we complete the pass by the wingback, it is usually a great big gain.

We can throw the *Throwback Pass* to the blocking back off of the 18 Pass where the quarterback pulls up quickly. The tight end will run a drag route. The blocking back will slip out in the flat on the quick side. We have had good yardage on this play.

The last pass diagrammed is a *Screen Pass*. The diagram illustrates how it is executed.

We do not have a jillion pass routes or a jillion pass plays; we have the ones we think we need. And we have never gone in a game without being able to throw these.

Let me say one more time again—moving the end over in our single-wing offense has done more for our offense than *any* other thing. The end over is the *key*. We ran for a long time the balanced-line single wing where we split the left end some, but when we decided to have an end over, it made our strong-side running game better, it made our passing game better, and it gave us a good reverse and counter attack. Those good pass routes back to the quick side help too.

We explained earlier that our philosophy is to have a strong running game, but you also have to throw the football to win. The key is to throw it when you *want* to, not when you *have* to. We are not like the teams that just go totally pass happy and throw it fifty or sixty times a game. We will explain more in the strategy section of this book. All of these plays have given us a good passing game.

Everyone has to block except the split end; he just has to be a runner down that field. When we grade film, he gets a one hundred percent if somebody goes with him and covers him; it is as if he had blocked a man down every play. This is basically our passing game for the single-wing offense.

Causes of Interceptions

1. <u>Do not throw off balance</u>. Throwing off balance is responsible for more interceptions than all other factors in the passing game. Off-balance passing is often caused by poor protection, leaving the cup, and throwing off of the wrong foot. It can also be caused by simply throwing too late, allowing rushers to get in on you. Of one thing you can be sure: if your body is not moving *forward* as the ball is thrown, you can only get the ball to the target by counteracting the loss of body motion with increased trajectory of the ball (lofting the ball). Increased lofting of the ball means more time for the defense to cover, and the answer is an obvious one—an interception.

2. <u>Do not throw over linebackers</u>; throw between them. To throw over them is to soften the pass so that a deep man can intercept.

3. <u>Do not throw a long pass short</u>. Any long pass thrown short will in theory be thrown to the deep defender. Most overthrown passes will result in incompletions.

4. <u>Never throw a short pass long</u>. The short pass should never be thrown above number high. Hit them in the numbers or belt region.

5. All receivers must run correct patterns and assume that each pass will be thrown to them.

6. <u>Do not use desperate heaves to get you out of trouble</u>, for they will simply get you into more trouble.

7. Do not throw deep passes on obvious passing downs, for the defense will be waiting for you. Short patterns, running passes, and sweeps will serve your purpose much better.

8. Do not throw from a wide stance, for you must bring your feet together before you throw, which will cause you to pass the ball late. If you remain in a wide, spread-out stance, you will under throw your target.

9. Do not ignore passing percentages, for if you are going to have one out of fourteen passes intercepted, make sure that your gamble has enough of a TD chance to offset these odds.

10. Learn to "zip" that football! Do not throw a soft, pretty pass. It is far more important that you "hum" that ball in there and let our receivers learn to be good receivers. On quick, short passes, always throw at a low target. Do not let the ball sail. On long passes, where the receiver is running away from you, that is when you put some loft on the ball. Practice squaring those shoulders on the running pass and work for a quick release on all passes.

18 Pass Blocking Offense Against the Odd and Even

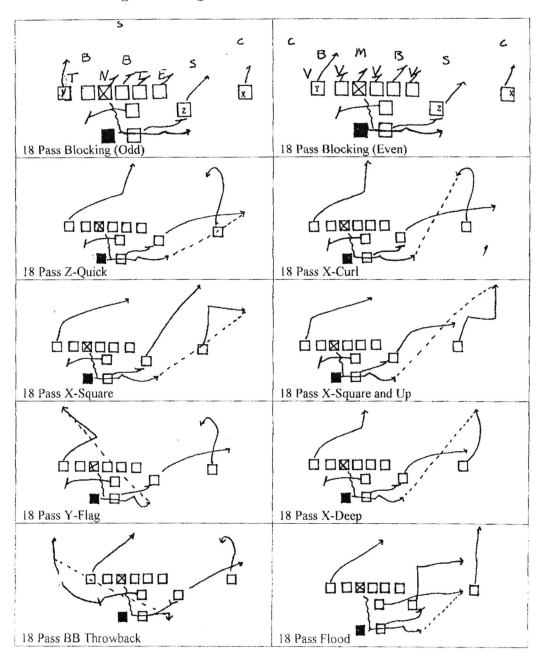

18 Pass Blocking (Odd)

18 Pass Blocking (Even)

18 Pass Z-Quick

18 Pass X-Curl

18 Pass X-Square

18 Pass X-Square and Up

18 Pass Y-Flag

18 Pass X-Deep

18 Pass BB Throwback

18 Pass Flood

Play Pass

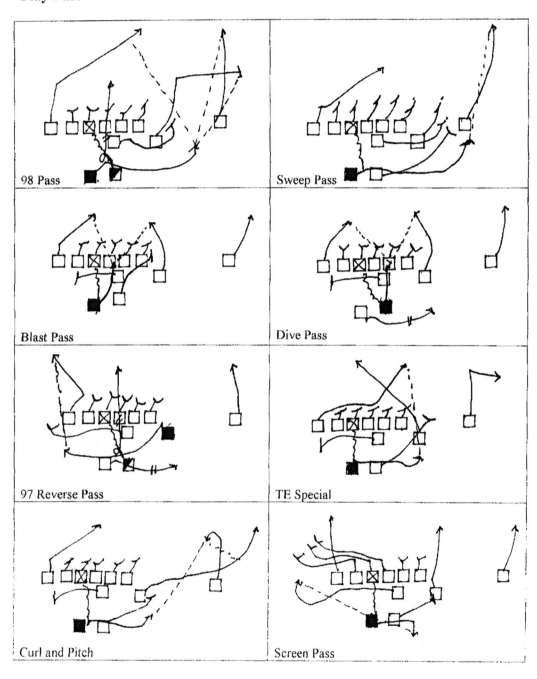

"98 Pass"

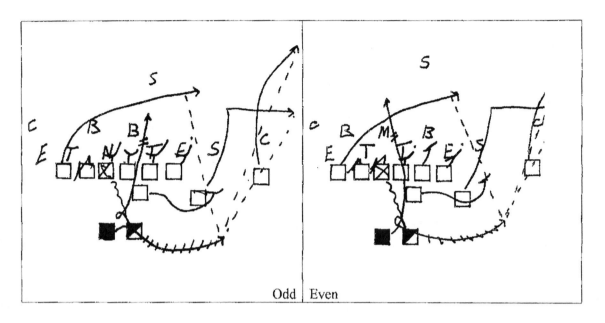

Odd | Even

Chapter 12

Variations and Special Plays

Variations of the Single Wing

The single wing has other series to run besides what we run. We run the Teen Series (our tailback series, strong side), Forty Series (tailback series, quick side), Thirty Series (direct series for the fullback), and the Ninety Series (fullback spinner—our deception in our offense). But we have run a thing we call the Draw Series (the 80 series). There are four plays—*88 Pass* off the draw fake, *84* (fake to the fullback and tailback keeps through the four hole), *80 Trap* (up the middle blocked like our 40 and 90 Trap), and *87 Reverse* (blocked like our 97 Reverse).

We have not run these plays the last few years. The Draw Series is the one that most teams are running off the spread today. But that was a good series for us.

The single wing also has something called the Buck Lateral Series. The fullback takes the snap and gets up into the line. The blocking back turns around down low. The fullback hands him the ball as he goes up through the middle of the line. Or he would keep it on a trap play. Or if he gave it to the blocking back, the blocking back could pitch it out to the tailback on an option play or hand it off to the wingback on a reverse.

There are some good things in the single wing you can run. But you can get so much offense that you cannot execute it all. We always tried to keep our cut to never more than twenty plays in our offense. If you run that right and left, that makes forty plays. That is a lot of offense. I will say this, maybe because I am not very smart, but I never did get in a ball game and need a play that we did not have. I imagine there might have been one we needed that I did not know anything about, but we never thought we needed anything we did not have. We could do everything we needed from our series. The single wing does have some things besides what we do.

Special Plays

People used to call special plays "trick" plays. Some of them are pretty tricky. Some of them are no longer legal. We would run some. These are hard to diagram on paper, because you have to explain them. That is almost like writing another book.

I will give you the names of several and how we used them. If you are interested in any of them, you can contact me, and I will get them to you or show them to you on film or sit down and explain them.

We ran a play called the *Whisper Play*. We would go to the line of scrimmage. Just as we would get down, our tight end would rise up and look back at our tailback like he did not know what the snap count was, and our blocking back would run over to him really still and whisper to him. While he was whispering to him, the other team's defense was sitting there watching him whisper, and we would snap the ball to our tailback and run a sweep on the right side. We did that on extra points sometimes.

We ran an *End-Around Play* where we would run our 97 Reverse. You come around the quick side. Our tight end would come back around and pick it up and run it to the strong side.

We ran the old *Statue-of-Liberty Play* where our tailback would rise up like he was going to throw it and hand the ball behind him to a back coming by. The spread teams do that today.

We had a *Quick-Kick Reverse*. The tailback would back up really quick, snap the ball, and fake by putting the ball behind him on his hip. He would go through the kicking motion, and the wingback would pick it off and run the reverse on it. The best thing that ever happened off of that was one night when we did it *twice* to a team. The next week they were waiting for it, so he just backed up really quick, went through the kicking motion, put the ball behind his back, and kept it there. The wingback came by and faked a reverse, and all eleven of the other team's defense were chasing our wingback when our fullback ran down the right sideline for about fifty yards!

We had a thing we call the *Hammer Play*. Only one back takes the snap. The others are played in the gaps on the strong side—blocking back, wingback, and fullback. We just out-man the other team on that side and run a power play.

There are many other trick plays. One of them I cannot even explain in writing! If you are interested, contact me.* In recent years college teams like Boise State have been out there running trick plays and can beat a great team like Oklahoma. They execute them well. A lot of people call that garbage football. One of the greatest coaches I ever knew made a statement that anybody you can beat by fooling, you can beat anyway. I am not sure that is true, but we will run some trick plays every now and then. It is fun for the players, and it keeps the practice from being so dull.

If you are interested in receiving more information or help from Coach Anderson, you may contact him at 972-904-0187.

Chapter 13

Practice/Work-out Schedule

Day	Date	Offense	Defense
1. Stretching 2. Cally 3. Starts 4. Springs	Time	Time 1. Dummies 2. Tackling 3. Team kicking 4. Punt return	Agility
1st Quarter	Individual	Group	**2nd Quarter**
	Time Half	Time Half	
3rd Quarter	Individual-Team	Team	**4th Quarter**
	Time	Time	
Specialty			**Comments**

Chapter 14

Strategy and Philosophy

You win football by running the football. We are in a pass-happy generation, but you win by running.

This chapter is about strategy. In our system of single-wing football, we feel we have a formation from which you can run the ball well or throw the ball well. We can also make long, sustaining drives and control the football, run the clock, and keep the ball away from teams that have a good offense. Also, a big part of this system and philosophy we believe in is to manage the clock. A lot of people think this is dull football. They used to call it "three yards and a cloud of dust." It is not three yards. Sometimes it is one, sometimes it is sixty. We need to make long, sustaining drives. We think that is important.

In my years of coaching, I observed many, many times that the people who won year after year consistently (not necessarily the championship every year), were coached by coaches who had a system they believed in. I saw one who had the system of the wishbone. Other people would not want the wishbone for anything, but they consistently won with it. I saw two teams that won with the wing T. They had a system, stayed with it, and consistently won with it. You have to get something you do believe in, something you know, and stay with it. Start your young seventh and eighth graders off learning that and bring them up through it all the way, and you will be able to have a consistent and winning program. In our case, we believed in the single wing, and that was the thing we were going to do.

I was a head coach for thirty-three years, and for twenty of those years we ran the pure single wing. We ran it partially in other years with the wing T, but I do not count that. In our twenty years of running the single wing, we were consistent. If we ever got out of it, we would come back to it, and the next year it would put us in the championship race, and we would go to the play-offs again. You have to have something you believe in and not jump around from place to place.

You have to also convince and hire people who will believe in the philosophy you have. All young coaches have ideas. I do not want to squelch those, and I have answered many, many questions about why we did not do this or that. You have to have people who are loyal and who work and who believe exactly like you do. That is what made it successful.

People say that offense wins games, and defense wins championships. That is true to an extent. I do not recall ever having a championship football team that did not have a good defense. But you have to have all phases of the game. You have to have a good offense, a good defense, and a sound, solid, good kicking game—kick offs, kick-off returns, spread punts, punt returns, extra points, and field goals. Year after year you may be stronger in one than the other. But all of those things go together. We believed in our system. We believed we could take the football and keep it. I like that idea of keeping it away from the other team. If they have a great passer, great receiver, and great running back, you can get the ball and keep it, and those players are just standing on the sideline drinking Gatorade! They are not out there playing offense and giving your defense problems.

Another thing I believe in strongly is clock management. I want to know how much time is on the clock. We are going to work that clock to our advantage. Some people have said before, and I might have fallen into this category at one time, that their idea of the perfect football game was to score one time in each quarter and take eight minutes to do it each time. We have kept the ball eight minutes, even nine minutes and fifty-two seconds once, but you do not get to do that all the time. Penalties and mistakes sometimes alter it. You have to be able to throw the football when you *want* to and not when you *have* to. Anytime the teams are anywhere near or equal in talent, lots of time passing will make the difference. It has won lots of big games for us.

Another thing you have to teach your team is not to let weather be a factor in whether we win or lose. Some people like to play in the rain, and some do not. I never was that concerned about it.

In fact, the wind bothered me as a player more than the rain did. It also bothered me sometimes as a coach when trying to decide whether to kick off or get the ball the second half. (That was before you could defer.) You have to prepare your players for the weather. If you are a playoff football team, you are probably going to play in some bad weather.

As we used to say, "I want to be an overcoat football coach." Anybody can coach in those nice slacks or those shorts and T-shirts during the regular season. But I want to be an overcoat coach, coaching when it is very, very cold. You have to convince your football team that rain will *help* our offense, because if we snap the ball and fumble it, we are at least four yards back there, and we can fall on it. I do not know if I can prove that or not, but that is what we try to get across to our players.

Also, cold weather is where we want to play. Playing in cold weather means either you are playing for the playoffs, or you are in the playoffs. I have played the last game of the season three different times when in was snowing really lightly, and it was very cold. The other team had a big heater on the sideline, and they all had those long, sideline jackets. We bought some great sideline jackets, and our football team refused to wear them, because they thought the coats were a sign of weakness. I noticed all the *coaches* had one on though. I was not trying to prove we were not cold, because everybody knew we were. But we made it so that cold weather was not a factor. We will play in the cold, when it is wet, when the wind is blowing, or whatever it is. That is just part of being a good football team. Cold weather does not get you beaten. Anybody cold? "No sir!"

The last part of strategy is that when you get your system, believe in it and stay with it. Don't panic when things go wrong during the ball game. Stay positive with the players. I have seen people chew players out so badly. We have all been guilty of jumping on them and correcting them when they make a mistake. But let us stay positive with them, because they are the ones who are going to have to believe we can do this no matter what the score is. And the last quarter will belong to us. That is just a coaching point you have to get across. You cannot preach that and not practice it.

One final word. Paul said it best in Philippians 4:13, "I can do all things through Christ who strengthens me."

Appendix A

Index of Abbreviations

Offense

TE	Tight end
QG	Quick-side guard
C	Center
SG	Strong-side guard
IT	Inside tackle
OT	Outside tackle
SE	Split end
TB	Tailback
FB	Fullback
BB	Blocking back
WB	Wingback

Defense

N	Nose guard
T	Tackle
E	End
V	Down lineman
B	Linebacker
M	Middle linebacker
S	Safety
C	Cornerback

Appendix B

Biography of Bobby Anderson

Coach Bobby Anderson knew he wanted to be a football coach from the time he was in the fifth grade. In thirty-three years as a head coach he earned well over 200 wins. In the twenty years that he ran the single wing, his record of 152 wins, 47 losses, and five ties still stands tall. He is a coach whose blood is football and whose life is teamwork. When referring to his team, players, or staff, he never says, "I" or "My" but always, "We" or "Our." He wants to win, and he has with the single wing! He taught his players that teamwork comes before winning. And character is a big part of that. Though many people believe that football develops character, Coach Anderson says it doesn't; it exposes character. He never talked of winning, but winning came as a result of the teamwork he built. And the single wing helped build teamwork by allowing even the smaller players to participate. Coach Anderson believes that when you get the fundamentals right and get the players to believe in themselves and each other, the winning will take care of itself.

Bobby Anderson graduated from San Augustine High School in San Augustine, Texas. He played football at Louisiana Tech University as quarterback and lettered in football and track, graduating in 1957. Coach Anderson coached football for forty-three years in Texas, thirty-three of which as a head coach. His teams in public school were successful in Class A, 2A, 3A and 4A; they were also successful at the middle school level. His teams won or tied fifteen district championships in the days when only one team could go to the playoffs. He was the assistant coach at Forney High School and Lakehill Preparatory School for eight years. During the last five years of his coaching career, he was the head football coach at Providence Christian School of Texas with an almost perfect record. In those five years, three of his teams were undefeated and one team lost only one game.

Recognized as Coach of the Year in his district or region eight times, Coach Anderson served on the Texas High School Coaching Association Board of Directors in 1971-73 and on the All-Star Selection Committee in 1972. He was inducted into the Texas High School Coaches Hall of Honor in 2002—a career honor. He is married and has two children—son Don with wife Cindy and daughter Shari with husband Jeff. His three grandchildren are Nicki, Rob, and Alex. Anderson currently resides in Rowlett, Texas.

This is how Coach Anderson coached—one hand on the shoulder, the other hand making his communication expressive, all with the cowboy hat sitting tall! This is Coach Anderson!

LaVergne, TN USA
03 December 2010

207231LV00003B/118/P

9 781609 575939